HOW TO MEET
A Gorgeous Girl

Also by Marjorie Sharmat

HOW TO MEET
A Gorgeous Girl

A NOVEL BY
MARJORIE SHARMAT

DELACORTE PRESS/NEW YORK

Published by
Delacorte Press
1 Dag Hammarskjold Plaza
New York, N.Y. 10017

Manufactured in the United States of America

Library of Congress Cataloging in Publication Data

Sharmat, Marjorie Weinman.
How to meet a gorgeous girl.

Summary: Mark Gardner's romance with Meg Low-
man is actually impeded, not enhanced, by his new
book *How to Meet a Gorgeous Girl*.
I. Title.
PZ7.S5299How   1984   [Fic]
ISBN 0–385–29324–0
Library of Congress Catalog Card
Number: 83–14365

For my sister Rosalind
with love and appreciation
for pegging me right

1

At first Meg couldn't believe that *he* wanted to meet her. But there he was standing across the counter from her again. She had been selling cosmetics for five mornings in Harriman's Department Store. *He* had come in the second morning and the third and the fourth, and here he was again. He was tall, very attractive, and soft-spoken, and if she had seen him anywhere else, any-where *logical*, she would have wanted to see him again.

She had to be polite. He was a customer. He had bought something from her every day. How much more could he buy? Maybe he was here to return something.

"Your sister didn't like the Glossy Glow you bought on Tuesday?" she asked.

"No, it was great."

"Then your mother wasn't crazy about the Crinkle Concealer you got her on Wednesday, I guess. It doesn't conceal everything."

"That was great, too."

"Then it must have been the Flaw-Away you bought for your aunt's flaws yesterday that didn't work?"

"That was great."

"So?"

"So, you have a great memory. About all those products, I mean."

"Can I help you with something else?"

"What have you got?"

"What do you need?"

"I have this cousin who, well, her hair isn't all that it could be."

"Sorry, I don't have hair products at this counter."

"Well, her skin isn't so great either. You have plenty of stuff here for bad skin, don't you?"

"What's wrong with her skin?"

"I think it's her pores. They're too large or too small."

"I'm only here temporarily and all I know about pores is that we have something for opening them and something for closing them. The regular cosmetics person will be back at the end of the month, and she's an expert. Can you wait that long?"

"Almost a whole month? Great!"

"What?"

"Nothing. Thanks."

Then *he* walked away.

Meg watched him. He had a nice walk. But why didn't he say something normal like "When I saw you behind this counter, I knew I had to meet you. There's a long, hot summer ahead of us and I want to go swimming with you, and picnicking with you, and hiking with you. I want to rescue you from behind this cosmetics counter."

She was dying to tell her mother about him. Or her friend Rhonda. But her mother would ask, "Were you slouching when he first saw you?" Her mother always said that when you slouch nobody notices anything else about you.

Meg decided that when she got home she would call Rhonda. Rhonda always congratulated herself on having insight into situations.

Maybe *he* would be back in the meantime.

He didn't come back. It was a good thing, Meg thought. She was busy with customers who really wanted something.

At noon Meg left the store and went home. The job was only part-time, but Meg knew she was lucky to have it. When school let out, she had applied for a summer job at Harriman's as a stock girl. She was hired part-time, and she spent one month as a stockperson, as her supervisor had called it. "I'm having a stockperson summer," Meg had told Rhonda. But then an opening turned up in the cosmetics department behind the Young Faces counter. They needed a replacement for a month. Meg always used Young Faces products. She knew the merchandise. "Know the merchandise and you know everything" was a behind-the-scenes saying at Harriman's. When Meg stepped behind the counter for the first time, she felt it was her turf. If she did well, maybe they would want her back next summer. Maybe someday she would be a store executive, and she would tell all incoming employees how she started as a stockperson.

When Meg got home, she made herself lunch, ate quickly, and then called Rhonda. Meg had known Rhonda since they were both eight years old. They had met on the sidewalk in front of Meg's house. "I'm going to be a lion tamer when I grow up," Rhonda had announced. "It's a good line of work and it has lots of fringe benefits."

Rhonda was always like that. Sure of herself, and knowing things that Meg didn't know. Rhonda's confidence and Meg's lack of it had drawn them together. Meg was always confiding things in Rhonda, and Rhonda told her what they really meant. But sometimes Rhonda would just kid her and not tell her anything. "What if you were on a desert island and I wasn't?" Rhonda had said one day. "You would get yourself off the island, and you would think I did it by myself without Rhonda."

"I'll remember that the next time I'm stranded on a desert island," said Meg.

"On the other hand," Rhonda had said, "you're the only one who can rescue me from an increasingly boring life. So don't hesitate to impart anything of a scandalous nature."

"This isn't exactly scandalous," Meg thought as she waited for Rhonda to answer the phone. "But Rhonda's so hard up for excitement this summer she'll listen to anything."

"Hello."

"Rhonda?"

"Is that a question? So, how's life at the cosmetics counter?"

"Listen, there's this guy, he looks about sixteen or seventeen, and he's been at my counter four days in a row buying stuff."

"For *himself?*"

"No, silly. For his sister and then his mother and then

his aunt. But he didn't actually buy anything today. He just talked to me and left."

"What does he look like that the women in his family need all this makeup?"

"He looks like a soap opera star. Like Rick on *Tomorrow's Yesterday*."

"Allllllllright! Maybe he is. Do you know anything about him?"

"I never saw him before this week. So he's either new in town or he goes to a different high school."

"Maybe he's just a summer visitor."

"Could be."

"So anyway, what are you going to do about Rick?"

"His name isn't Rick. I mean, it most likely isn't Rick."

"Let's call him Rick. It's more fun that way. Come on. This is desperation summer so far. Nothing has happened, and we've been out of school over a month. Of course if I had an imagination like yours, I'd be all set."

"But it's not my imagination. He wants to meet me. I know it. I mean *really* meet me."

"He'd better hurry up. Does he know you'll only be at Harriman's till the end of the month?"

"I told him that today."

"Poor Rick. He'll kill himself."

"I'm hanging up, Rhonda."

"I'm going to watch *Tomorrow's Yesterday* and see what Rick is doing. If he takes poison, I'll let you know."

"Good-bye, Rhonda."

Suddenly Meg was tempted to watch *Tomorrow's Yesterday*. Maybe it would be like watching *him*. Anyway, it would be company. Her mother was busy typing in another room. Her mother wrote cookbooks. One of these days someone was going to publish them. That's what her mother always predicted. Her father was away again on a business trip to Japan. He was an executive with a shoe company.

Meg went to her room to watch TV. Her parents had given her the set for her fifteenth birthday last month. She had hinted for two years.

The sweet music for *Tomorrow's Yesterday* came on. Every now and then Meg watched the show. When she was home sick from school she watched it. She watched it from time to time during vacations. Half of the girls at school were in love with Rick. Meg didn't want to be in love with anyone she could turn on and off with a switch.

Rick was involved with two women on the show. One was older, one was younger. Rick walked around with one lock of hair falling over his forehead. That was his trademark. His face flashed on the screen. He was gazing at the older woman. He *did* look like the guy who kept coming by her counter. Not exactly. They weren't the same person, that was for sure. But Meg almost expected Rick to say to the older woman, "That Crinkle Concealer does wonders for you."

Meg turned off the TV. She thought about her summer. It was at midpoint. Forget the first half, the glory of being a stockperson. Now she had a clean, bright fantastic job behind the cosmetics counter. And there was a guy showing up four days in a row. Did he like her? He probably didn't like her. He probably wouldn't show up again. Would he?

2

"I don't care if she slouches, she's gorgeous!"

Mark Gardner was walking in the mall with his friend Toolie Drake.

"Sorry, Mark. You told me to look at her so I looked," said Toolie. "She *is* nice. I was just kidding. So what were you two talking about today?"

"Face blusher, under-eye concealer, and flaw eraser. Also, my cousin with pores."

"You didn't buy any more junk, did you? I won't—repeat *won't*—return any more of that guck. My manhood's on the line. Besides, they're getting to know me. Every day you buy. Every day I return. I wouldn't mind if it were a radio or a watch or something. But this stuff is *embarrassing*. How can you buy it?"

"What's my alternative? She doesn't work in radios and watches. I didn't seek out that counter. I was just wandering around the store Tuesday and there she was. I mean, there *she* was. So beautiful behind those cosmetics. That long black hair. Those blue eyes. Blue like cornflowers."

"Have you ever seen a cornflower?"

"No, but I've certainly heard about them. Anyway, I walked back and forth, back and forth, watching her while she waited on customers. Then I circled her counter and got views of her from all angles. I've never seen anyone like her. The rest was inevitable."

"The rest was ridiculous. Why didn't you just go up and introduce yourself?"

"She might have told me to get lost. But she has to talk to a customer."

"So where has it gotten you?"

"Nowhere."

"So forget it. Or else make your own returns. That lady who replaces her at noon—the one I return the stuff to—well, she's got one of those faces that smiles in the front but is busy taking inventory in the back. Know what I mean? She's on to me."

"I can't give up."

"Wise up, Mark. The world is full of girls that guys can't meet. Accept it. They pass you on the street and never look sideways. Or they walk toward you and keep their eyes straight ahead. They stand in front of you in lines while you examine every silken strand of their wonderful hair, but they don't know you're there. If they happen to turn around, they fix their gaze on something directly over your head. They sit in clusters at the beach and wiggle their toes in the sand while you, the invisible guy, walk by. I know what it's like to be unseen, ignored, and not there when I'm actually there. There's one girl at school who examines every one of her fingernails sort of microscopically every time she sees me go by and she doesn't raise her eyes again until I've safely passed. I turned around once and I caught her looking up after I'd gone by. So you see, pal, I understand. Now, let's not waste the day. I have to buy a music book for my father."

"I wish she worked in books. You can have a real conversation with someone in books."

"Well, she doesn't. Hey, stop. We're going past the bookstore."

Mark and Toolie walked into the bookstore. "This may take a while," said Toolie. "He wants a book on cellos, and the book has a dark green cover and that's all I remember about it. I left the name of the book at home."

"Take your time," said Mark. "I'll browse."

"The cosmetics books are over there," said Toolie.

"You're a riot."

Mark wandered around the bookstore. He picked up books and thumbed through them. He liked the nonfiction books the best. They divided the world into categories. They made the world manageable. How to do this. How to do that.

Did people really wonder how to raise a well-adjusted cat? Would they really want to know how to decorate a bathroom ninety-nine different ways if they only had one or two bathrooms? Would they want to know how to meet a gorgeous girl?

"What?"

Mark stopped. *How to Meet a Gorgeous Girl.* There it was. The answer to a real problem. *His* problem.

Mark picked up the book. The title *How to Meet a*

Gorgeous Girl was in large gold script, diagonally scrawled across a bright blue cover. The author's name was near the bottom of the cover. Between the title and the author's name was a photograph of a phony-looking gorgeous girl. She looked as if she wasn't willing to meet anybody back. She was beyond the reach of mortal man.

Mark turned the book over. On the back was a picture of the author who, on the other hand, looked as if he were anxious to reach everyone. His face leaped out, eager and alert. He was wearing an open shirt with the hair on his chest showing. There was a beseeching look about him.

"He's begging me to buy his book," thought Mark. "And Miss Snooty Face on the cover is saying 'Catch me if you can.' What a pair."

Mark opened the book. "I'll just glance at it for free. That'll serve both of them right."

Mark flipped pages. He started to read at random.

If you're a normal male, you've faced rejection over and over. Don't believe your friends who tell you *they* haven't. They've all yearned for the unobtainable.

He flipped more pages.

So that's what can happen when you don't know what you're doing. You think you're Mr. Macho. That's your first mistake and you don't know that you've made it. You, sir, are an amateur.

Mark flipped a few more pages.

That was strategy number three. If properly imple-
mented, you are now acquainted with that girl of your
dreams. You've done it. Congratulations! But if
strategy number three wasn't for you—and have
confidence that only *you* know *yourself*—then skip it
and go on to strategy number four.

Mark looked at the front flap of the book. The price
was fifteen dollars and ninety-five cents, but it was
crossed off, with a new price of only two dollars and
ninety-five cents printed beneath it. He had the money.
Toolie had gotten the refund for the Flaw-Away, the
flaw eraser that the gorgeous girl had sold him yesterday
morning. It was providential! Fate meant for him to
buy this book. He turned to the back flap. It told about
the author, the man whose picture was on the back of
the book. He was some kind of doctor. He might be
some kind of nut, Mark figured. But it was hard to put
the book back on the table and walk away from it. It
might be the only way he could meet the gorgeous
girl behind the counter. He opened the book for another look. He saw the word *grateful*. There was a
whole chapter on how to make a girl feel grateful to
you.

"Whatcha reading?" Toolie was back. He was carrying a bag.

"Look at this," said Mark, holding up the book. "It's a
lot of garbage—hot air—isn't it?"

"Don't know. Haven't read it."

"You're not laughing over it?"

"Nope."

"It's something a person could take seriously?"

"Maybe."

"Should I buy it with the refund money from the Flaw-Away?"

"Sure, if it means you won't have any money left to buy more of that junk."

Mark clutched the book. He was going to buy it! And now that he was buying it, now that it was going to be his, it seemed like an ally.

When they were back in the mall, Mark asked, "Did you find your book?"

"Yeah, there were stacks of copies. Imagine stacks of books about the cello."

"There was only one copy of my book. It was marked down."

"Sure. It's probably a dog."

"A dog? The book I bought is a dog? Why didn't you tell me that before I bought it?"

"Some dogs are lovable. Anyway, why do you need a book like that? If I could sing and play the guitar like you, I'd go right up to that girl and make beautiful music."

"Oh, sure. Right in the middle of Harriman's Department Store. They'd cart me away. Some day when I have my own group, girls will pay to watch me."

Mark and Toolie walked along the mall. Mark pictured himself as the leader of his own group. He would be playing in the mall near the center fountains. Sometimes the mall featured little musical groups on special occasions. A crowd would gather. The gorgeous girl would be in it. She would be watching him. She would be listening. She might fall in love with him. Girls often fall in love with guitar players just like that. No, it wouldn't happen that way with her. She was too great just to fall for someone so easily. But with a little help, anything is possible.

Mark looked down at his new book and smiled.

3

"I'll have ten tubes of Flaw-Away, please."

He was back! Meg knew he would be back. Too bad Rhonda wasn't here to see it. It was Monday, the beginning of a new week.

"*Ten* tubes? That will cover an army of flaws."

"Yuh, well I have a lot of flawed relatives."

"Will that be cash again?"

"Of course."

Meg rang up the sale. She was thinking, "He wants me to think he's a big shot. Rich or something. That's why he's doing this. What a dumb way to try to impress me."

"Thank you," said Mark. "Have a nice morning."

"You're welcome." Meg watched him make his way through the shoppers. She sighed. "I can't stand kids who flaunt their money. He's probably some rich, spoiled guy who goes to private school. He's bought thirteen items from me so far. That comes to over forty dollars. It's probably a small fraction of his weekly allowance."

Mark rushed into the mall where Toolie was waiting for him in front of a record store. "I did it!" said Mark. "And now it's your turn. That is, as soon as she leaves and the lady takes over at noon."

"I said I'd never return another thing to the cosmetics counter," said Toolie. "Not one more thing."

"But it's your money I used. Thanks for lending it to me. I wish *I* could save up all that money from my allowance. Anyway, it's no sweat for you to get it back. You said the lady smiles all through the returns. Don't lose sight of our goal. That gorgeous girl is now *grateful* to me for buying all that stuff. I've done wonders for her sales record."

"What about her returns record?" asked Toolie. "Did you ever think about that?"

"She'll never find out the stuff was returned, will she? That would be the pits. I figure by the time I go up to her counter tomorrow, she'll be thrilled to see me. I'm turning her into a successful businesswoman. Tomorrow is when I make my move. I'll introduce myself. The book says, first *gratitude*, then *introduction*. The gratitude paves the way. I read the entire 'How to Make Her Grateful' chapter of the book. I figured that was the chapter meant for me. It said to do subtle but significant favors for her."

"Some subtle," said Toolie.

"It's just about twelve. Here, take the stuff. It's ten tubes of Flaw-Away. Just so you know what you're returning. Now go and do it and you'll have your money back in your pocket before you know it. It came to just under thirty-two dollars, including tax, the exact amount I borrowed. I knew it would. I'm careful with your money."

"You owe me," said Toolie. "For favors like this, you'll be in my debt for life."

Mark and Toolie walked back into Harriman's Department Store. Toolie walked up to the cosmetics counter while Mark pretended to be busy in Shoes.

The lady was behind the cosmetics counter. "It will be over in a minute," thought Toolie. "Bless the cheery ladies of this world."

"Hi, there," said Toolie.

The cheery lady smiled. Then the smile froze.

Toolie put the bag of Flaw-Aways on the counter. "I'd like to return these, please."

"What again? You've been returning things constantly. Are you one of those chronic returners? I've never met a teen-ager who was a chronic returner. It's an age-related disease, and you're not the right age. Kids your age throw things away if they don't want them. And they've never heard of the word *quality*, so you can't be returning these products for lack of it. Is this a joke or something?"

"No, honestly."

"Just one moment, please."

The lady waved to someone. Toolie saw a woman walking toward them. She looked like an authority figure, one of those ladies with a mind closed to everything except her particular mission. Toolie knew *he* was her mission. He wanted to run. When she got closer, Toolie saw that she was one of those perfectly dressed, perfectly made-up people who look more like a product than a person.

"This is our cosmetics department manager, Ms. Selwyn. And this is the young man I've been telling you about. He's our dauntless returner."

Ms. Selwyn arched a perfect eyebrow. "What seems to be the problem with our merchandise?" she asked.

Toolie winced. Ms. Selwyn looked like a professional interrogator.

"I'm entitled to one phone call," said Toolie. He grabbed the bag from the counter and ran.

He expected someone to grab him by the collar.

Toolie ran into the mall. Mark followed him. "What happened?" Mark asked.

"They were waiting for me. It was an ambush of sorts. And you are now the proud owner—the permanent owner—of ten tubes of Flaw-Away. And you owe me thirty-two bucks."

"Rats! Just when I was about to activate my plan."

"Look, maybe this girl isn't worth it. What if she's got a boyfriend? You don't know anything about her."

"I know she doesn't go to Portland High or I'd have noticed her."

"Okay. Big deal. She doesn't go to Portland. So what?"

"So I keep thinking about kissing her. How do you suppose it feels? The farther away she is from me, the more I think about being close to her. It's bugging me. I'm going to read that book from page one. I shouldn't have plunged in at Chapter Three. That's what went wrong."

"The guy who wrote it looks like a slick character. You don't want to be a slick character, do you?"

"Anything that works."

4

It was bums' day at Meg's house. Meg didn't want her mother to know that she called it that, but what else was it when her mother invited four personally selected bums to her house for lunch to taste her food? Every Monday for months, Mrs. Lowman had been inviting seedy people to sample her newest concoctions. She was determined to try out every recipe that was going into her latest cookbook. Her friends and acquaintances were tired of being food samplers. "I need an ongoing scientific sampling," said Mrs. Lowman. "I need eaters I can depend upon, not this random eat and run. But more important than that, I can make a tangible contribution to their lives. A home-cooked meal every Monday."

Slowly Meg's mother had acquired a clientele of bums. Rhonda called them "the seedy needy." Mrs. Lowman picked them up in parks and soup kitchens, always careful to get acquainted with them first. "I choose the pathetic, not the violent," she said. The lunches became a Monday tradition. Occasionally something of value was missing from the house after a meal. But Meg's mother said, "I'm sure the poor soul needs it more than we do."

Someone had written a small article about these lunches in the local paper. After that, from time to time, Meg's mother received phone calls from people wanting to join her Monday group. She now had a backup list of bums.

When Meg got home from Harriman's, Randolph was in the living room. He was an ex-judge who had gotten into trouble with the law thirty years ago. Randolph liked to brag that he had accepted more bribes than any other judge in his county. "We kept a running tally," he boasted. "I always attracted the major donors." Randolph's favorite—perhaps only—outfit was a torn yellow shirt, frayed brown trousers, and an old blue belt that tried valiantly to hold the trousers up over an enormous pot belly. But he always wore a red bow tie, as if he were still trying to be a part of respectable society. Randolph was a regular. He was with the first group that had come to lunch, and he was back every Monday. Meg's mother liked him the best because "he's articulate about food."

Charlie and Burt were the other regulars. There was a constant turnover of the fourth diner. Today Charlie and Burt walked in together. They were usually together. The scent of stale tobacco, cat box filler, and muscatel seemed to hang over them permanently. "We're going back into biophysical science when the jobs open up again," Charlie always said solemnly.

"Yeah," Burt agreed. "If we settled for anything less, we'd be untrue to our destinies."

"Ain't it the truth," said Charlie.

There was a knock at the door. "The fourth diner," Meg thought. Her mother was doing last-minute things in the kitchen, so Meg answered the door.

A woman walked in. "Is this the place that's looking for a token tramp?" she asked.

"This here's the place," called Charlie. "What's your name?"

"Mrs. Carter Gish," said the woman. "And I think this idea is disgraceful."

"Then why yuh here?" asked Charlie.

"To make a statement."

"This ain't no statement place," said Burt. "We're here to eat."

The woman was wearing a gray suit with thin vertical stripes of white and had wispy brown hair and little darting eyes. She had a way about her that made Meg think of committees and speeches. Meg didn't want to see people like that during her summer vacation.

Meg's mother came into the room. "Welcome," she said to the woman. "I'm Trish Lowman and we're about to eat."

"I'm Mrs. Carter Gish. I read about your little luncheons. You're exploiting these people."

"I was under the impression I was feeding them."

"You're using them for your own purposes. Guinea pigs for a commercial enterprise. It's simply an extension of the soup kitchen mentality."

Mrs. Gish opened her pocketbook and took out three small white cards. She handed one to Randolph, one to Charlie, and one to Burt. "I'm from YWMTYT. You're Worth More Than You Think. We're a privately funded group established to help those people whose needs are falling through the cracks, so to speak. We deal with self-esteem, motivation, value assessment. How you feel about yourself can be more important than food on the table."

"I hadn't noticed," said Burt.

"We meet every Friday night. Our telephone number is on this card. Don't throw away the card after I leave. You may not think you need our services, but there'll come a time when you will. I know you circulate in the very bottom strata of society, that you inhabit the dumping ground of civilization, but gentlemen, you have *worth*."

Meg was getting angry. "You're insulting my mother," she said. "I think it would be a good idea if you left. Like right now."

"I've never been asked to leave premises before," said Mrs. Gish.

"Must have been an oversight," said Randolph. "If I still had the authority, I'd issue an eviction order right here on the spot."

"I came to explore this matter in a civilized manner." Mrs. Gish turned around and marched out.

"Thanks, Meg." Meg's mother hugged her. Meg loved her mother. She was the most generous person she knew, and Mrs. Gish was attacking her for it. Sure, her mother wanted to get a cookbook published. But she was kind to Randolph and Charlie and Burt. She never felt above them. "I accept them. They accept me," she said. It didn't bother her that they all had peculiar stories.

Meg went to her room. She rarely ate with her

mother's group. They were too busy discussing food. Besides, the cat box filler scent turned her off.

She started to think about *him* again. "Ten tubes of Flaw-Away. Who *is* he? Does he want me to be curious about him? I *am*. When he shows up at the counter tomorrow, I'll come right out and ask him what he wants."

Meg called Rhonda.

"Hello."

"*Ten* tubes of Flaw-Away."

"What?"

"That's right. It cost over thirty dollars in all. Tomorrow I'm going to find out what he's after."

"Can I watch?" Rhonda asked.

"I thought you'd never ask," Meg laughed. "You believe there's more to this than just a guy buying a bunch of makeup for relatives?"

"No. But I don't have anything else to do tomorrow."

"What enthusiasm."

"Do you know what you're going to say to him?"

"Yes. Who are you and what do you want?"

"That about covers it," said Rhonda.

5

"If only we got those summer jobs at Beefy Burg," said Toolie. He was sprawled out on the sofa in Mark's living room.

"Or the camp counselor jobs or the hardware store jobs or the playground maintenance jobs," said Mark.

"Anything that would have kept us out of Harriman's Department Store," said Toolie. "And into money."

"It says here to make yourself convenient and then play hard to get."

"What? Is that how you get a job?"

"I'm reading from the book. I'm beginning from the beginning. I'm at Chapter One. It says you should be where the girl is, and after she notices you, then you play hard to get."

"Does it tell you how to *meet* her? Isn't that what you're trying to do?"

"But not head-on, like a raging bull. That's a quote from Chapter One. First you have to work up to it. She has to want to meet *you*. It says you have to create that desire in her. Listen! 'You are out there in the cold, competitive world. The guy who succeeds in this climate is the one who seizes opportunities, who acts!! If you want to live a meek and mousy existence, you will. But don't you want more for yourself than that?'

"A meek and mousy existence?" said Mark. "This guy has never heard me play the guitar."

"You've got it," said Toolie. "He's a stranger and he's strange."

"Let's see what he says next," said Mark. "What have I got to lose? I've already bought the book. Listen. 'Basically you're a sensuous animal. Does that sound shocking? I meant it to be. And the girl you want to meet. Underneath it all she's probably an animal, too. Remember! She wants to meet you even if she doesn't know it yet.' "

Toolie sat up. "I've got bad news for you, Mark. You're not an animal. You're just an ordinary guy with an overflowing inventory of Flaw-Away."

"I don't think she's an animal," said Mark. "If she is, it's a fawn or something. She has big soft eyes."

"Why don't you forget this. You can't go back to the cosmetics counter, and that's your only link with her. It's finished. Face it."

"But the guy who wrote this book, *he* wouldn't quit. He says you have to seize opportunities, you have to act. That's pretty good advice, isn't it?"

"Yep. No quarrel with that. It's just that you don't have any opportunity to seize."

"I could create one. Like, I could follow her when she leaves at noon. How about it? Does it grab you?"

"Like a starving octopus. Please, Beefy Burg, call! Take me away from all of this. I'll work for nothing."

"There's a good view of the cosmetics counter from the shoe department. So we could go to the shoe department a little before noon and wait."

"For what?"

"For her to leave."

"Mark, we've been friends for a few years, right?"

"Right."

"And we've done some harebrained things together, okay?"

"Okay."

"Some of them were your harebrained ideas and some of them were my harebrained ideas."

"So?"

"So put them all together and they don't add up to anything as ridiculous as playing Sherlock Holmes in a shoe department. I don't want any part of it. Why don't you do it alone and tell me what happens?"

"The book says that if you're nervous about what you're doing, you should have a friend come along."

"The book says that?"

"Page seven."

"That slick guy thinks of everything."

"Yeah. I wonder why he was marked down from fifteen ninety-five."

Meg was at her counter a little early the next day. Ms. Selwyn was there to meet her. Meg didn't like Ms. Selwyn. She acted as if she had the entire world in her control. She acted as if cosmetics *were* the world.

"Meg," she said, "I know you're only temporary until

the end of the month, but we do expect a certain amount of good judgment even from our temps."

"Good judgment?"

"Yes. There's a young man who comes in and buys from you every morning. Then he or a friend of his—I haven't personally witnessed all of these transactions—returns everything after you leave. Mrs. Cogshell is always stuck with the returns. Is the purchaser a friend of yours?"

"No, I never saw him before last week. And I didn't know he was returning things."

Meg was trying to take in this information while keeping her head clear for Ms. Selwyn. So *that's* what he was doing with all that stuff he bought!

"Do you have any idea why he keeps doing this? Is he odd?"

"No, he seems very nice."

Ms. Selwyn stared at Meg. "Very nice? How would you know that?"

"Well, it's just an impression. He's a quiet type, and he has manners."

"Are you sure he isn't a friend of yours?"

"Are you calling me a liar?"

Meg knew she was on the brink of being fired. She wanted to keep this job. There was an excitement about it, about all the people, all the merchandise. It was almost theatrical. Rhonda was always talking about what they were going to "be." Rhonda wanted to be an anthropologist. Meg was beginning to think about retailing. But now as she looked at Ms. Selwyn's stony face, she felt that Harriman's and any future with Harriman's was slipping away from her.

Ms. Selwyn backed off. "We strive for happy employees, even temps," she said. "Naturally I'm not calling you a liar."

She walked away.

Meg let out a deep breath.

"I'll kill that guy if he comes back today."

6

"I can just smell success today," Mark said to Toolie as they picked up shoes and put them down.

"Does the book have a chapter on that?" asked Toolie. "The Olfactory Connection."

"It says that self-confidence is crucial. I memorized that section. 'Believe in yourself. You can do whatever you set out to do. You're the ruler of your own universe.'"

"Hogwash. Look around. Is this your universe?"

"Only temporarily. She'll be finished with her shift in a few minutes, and we'll follow her out of here. Like the book says, I've already created the desire for her to meet me. Now I have to be where the girl is, and after she notices me, I play hard to get."

"Just wonderful. I think there's already a foul-up in your plan. There's a girl talking to your dream girl, and it looks like they're friends. The other girl keeps hanging around. I bet she's waiting for her. She's trying samples, like she's killing time. What if they leave together?"

"We'll follow both of them."

"Why did I bother to ask?"

"So where is he?" asked Rhonda as she smeared some Glossy Glow on her wrist and held it up to the light.

"I don't know," said Meg. "I knew he'd come, but he didn't."

"Maybe he found someone else. Oh, well, these heavy romances break up every day. I'm getting hungry. Is it almost noon?"

"But I wanted you to meet him!"

"Why should I? You haven't."

"I was going to tell him off today. But now I won't have the chance."

"You're disappointed, aren't you."

Meg didn't want to admit that she was.

"It's time to go," said Rhonda.

"I have to wait for Mrs. Cogshell. She replaces me at noon. Never mind. Here she comes."

"Cheery looking, isn't she," said Rhonda.

"Yeah, but let's split before she asks me questions about *him*. Ms. Selwyn and she are buddies."

Meg waved to Mrs. Cogshell. Then she got her purse, and she and Rhonda quickly walked out of the store into the mall. They didn't notice that two people in the shoe department quickly dropped some shoes they were examining and started to follow them.

"I feel like a Beefy Burg," said Rhonda.

"Why not," said Meg.

Beefy Burg was halfway down the mall. It was

crowded. Meg and Rhonda had to wait in line to order. "This is inane," said Rhonda. "We should have gone to Healthburgers."

"That's usually busier," said Meg. "Health is big stuff these days."

Meg turned around. The line in back of her was getting longer. And at the very end, there *he* was!

"It's *him!*" Meg grabbed Rhonda's arm. "At the end of the line."

"Him? Oh, *him*, the cosmetics kid. Nice. Very nice. But he doesn't look anything like Rick. Rick doesn't have red hair."

"Not that guy. The one with him. Brown hair."

"Gotcha. Hey, he *does* look like Rick. What are you going to do about it?"

Meg shrugged.

"Aren't you going to tell him off about returning all the stuff?"

"How can I? He's not at my counter. It's the wrong place."

"He sees us staring at him. If he really likes you, he'll come up now."

"You think so?"

"Sure." Rhonda kept looking. "He's coming! I can't stand it." Rhonda turned away.

She felt a tap on her shoulder. "Hi there."

Rhonda turned around. *He* was talking to her. To *her*.

"I'm Mark Gardner."

"So?" said Rhonda.

"I'm an employee of Beefy Burg and I'm taking a random sampling of customers to ask why they chose Beefy Burg over other burgers."

"No, you're not," said Rhonda. "This is a pickup."

"Exactly. But it breaks the ice," said Mark. "Here's my I.D. card from high school. I'm a legitimate person. My friend back there, the one with the red hair, his name is Toolie Drake. And what is your name?"

"Don't tell him," said Meg. What nerve the guy had! First he was after her. Now he was after Rhonda.

Rhonda shrugged. "What's the difference. I'm Rhonda Schwartz and this is my friend Meg Lowman."

Meg glared at Mark. So he wasn't a stranger anymore. His name was Mark Gardner. But so what? He was after Rhonda. There was something about him at the cosmetics counter that seemed different. Almost sweet. But now he was just another one of those guys who come on too strong.

"It's been real," said Rhonda. And she turned her back on Mark.

"Yes, hasn't it," he said. He gave Meg a long look and he walked back to Toolie.

"I did it!" he said. "I got her to notice me and then I played hard to get. Just like the book said. I made a play for her friend. Oh, I found out her name. It's Meg Lowman. Do you think it fits her? I do."

"How should I know. Well, can we stop following her now?"

"I don't know. I don't have the book here."

Toolie groaned. "You don't deserve me for a friend. I'm too good for you. I'm patient and I'm wise. I'm old for my years."

"I'd like to see her reaction. What she does next."

"But we could be in this line forever. Besides, the book might not want you to stay here. Did you ever think of that?"

"I should have finished the chapter. Why didn't I finish it?"

"Let's talk it over at lunch. Someplace else."

"Okay. I've scored enough for one day anyway."

Mark and Toolie left the line. Mark turned back to look at Meg. Now that he had her name, he could find her address in the telephone book. He could find out all kinds of things about her. Thanks to the book, he was on his way. *How to Meet a Gorgeous Girl* wasn't a bargain. It was a steal.

Meg looked back at him. She hoped she would never see him again.

7

"I'm calling it *The Cookbook of the Five Diners*," said Meg's mother. "Kind of classy, huh? And I've written a little preface about my friends Randolph, Charlie, and Burt and about the Monday lunches. Your father thinks it's a wonderful idea."

"I do, too," said Meg. "But I hate to see you get your hopes up again. This is your ninth cookbook try. There are a lot of people out there writing cookbooks. I don't know why other people get published and you don't. Maybe they know somebody influential."

Meg wished *she* could help her mother. She wished she had the power. When she grew up she wasn't going to be like her mother. She wouldn't sit around and work on dream projects. She wouldn't be disappointed over and over again. She would be solid, competent, and successful. She would probably be dull, too.

Maybe she would become like Ms. Selwyn, faithful forever to the high standards of Harriman's Department Store. She would rule over a kingdom of Glossy Glow, Crinkle Concealer, and Flaw-Away. She would be safely enclosed in a creamy pink and white globe. She would never invite tramps to lunch.

Meg studied her mother. She had a glow about her of someone just on the brink of something wonderful. She never seemed to lose it.

"You wouldn't believe the morning I had," her mother said. "I couldn't get anything done. First Grandma Seeny phoned."

"Grandma? How's she adjusting to Serenity Village?"

"She isn't. She said she never would have moved to this town if she knew we'd find her a place in, uh, what did she call Serenity Village? Oh, Death Wish Manor. She said she's bored. I told her that when we all visit together a week from Sunday we'll have a nice long talk about it."

"A week from Sunday? Did she ask you to come sooner?"

"No. But she did say, 'Come with a moving van and move me.' We'll just have to get her out of that place, Meg."

"The phone call kind of wrecked your morning, huh?"

"*Two* phone calls. That Mrs. Gish phoned, too. She apologized for barging in the other day. But she says she still thinks it's demeaning to invite the fellows for a free lunch every Monday. She says I'm using them, plain and simple."

"*They* don't say that. They consider you a friend. They consider your project their project."

"The neighbors are talking, too. I can feel it. Dad's away for long stretches and here are these four men, or occasionally three men and one woman, coming to lunch every Monday. They're not exactly dressed in the latest fashions, and getting near Charlie and Burt isn't for everybody. But it's just been the greatest experience for me. This book is finished. But I'm not going to stop the lunches."

"Good for you, Mom."

"This will be the thickest book yet," said Meg's mother as she stacked the pages. "I used some recipes from each of the other eight books plus a bunch of new ones."

"Is that a good idea? If they were turned down before, won't they be turned down again?"

"I don't think anybody ever tried them, *tasted* them. I don't know what happens when a cookbook manuscript arrives at a publisher's. It's discouraging not even to know how things are handled, but I refuse to let it get me. Want to read my preface?"

Meg's mother held up a piece of paper.

"Sure."

Meg took the paper and started to read it.

Every Monday my four diners come to lunch. There's Randolph, Charlie, Burt, and a constantly changing fourth diner. Every Monday I serve them food made according to the recipes I have created for this book. We sit around, we sample, we talk. There is congeniality, companionship, caring. We are friends. Randolph is a retired judge, and Charlie and Burt are on sabbatical from the biophysical science field. The fourth diner changes from week to week but is often a wine-tasting expert with more work than he or she can handle. I am the fifth diner. I wrote this book.

Meg handed the paper back to her mother. "That's absolutely beautiful, Mom."

"Randolph said it was eloquent. And Charlie and Burt said amen. I'm going to put these pages in a box, write a covering letter, and send it out tomorrow. I just have the feeling that *this* one is going to make it. I'll be a cookbook author. A real one."

"Mom, please don't get so carried away again," said Meg. "Maybe a thousand cookbook manuscripts will arrive at that publisher's the day yours does."

Meg's mother smiled. "We're having a reverse conversation. What I mean is that you teen-agers are usually so boundlessly enthusiastic, and we middle-aged folks are decidedly earthbound."

"Well, maybe you're the teen-ager and I'm the middle-ager."

"You may have a point there," said Meg's mother.

Meg went to her room. "If I'm middle-aged," she thought, "then why am I angry over a teen-aged boy. Now I know his name. Big deal. I'm not going to let myself fall for someone who's after me and then isn't. He likes me, but he doesn't."

The telephone rang. Meg answered it.

"Have you simmered down?" It was Rhonda.

"I wasn't simmered up."

"You can't be mad because somebody's after you. You've been trying and trying to convince me that this guy was after you. Finally I saw the proof today and now *you* don't believe it."

"The proof was making a play for *you?*"

"Absolutely. Can't you see the pattern? That guy, he's a circler. He goes around and around his target, but he can't zoom in on it. I can't wait to see what he does next."

"*I* can."

8

You have successfully completed Chapter One. She now desperately wants to meet you.

Mark was reading from his book. "I fouled up," he said. "I wasn't supposed to meet her yet."

"I guess you're just an advanced student," said Toolie. Mark and Toolie were at Mark's house. *How to Meet a Gorgeous Girl* was open on the living room sofa.

"Have your folks seen this book?" asked Toolie.

"Naw. I keep it in my room. But you're talking as if it's X-rated or something."

"Maybe it is later on after you and the gorgeous girl are better acquainted. So what does Chapter Two say?"

"It tells how to prepare to meet. I have to skip ahead. Ah, Chapter Four."

"What happened to Chapter Three?"

"That was about making her grateful. It tells how to nail down the girl you really want to meet in Chapter

Two. I've already done that. Aren't you paying attention?"

"Not if I can help it."

"I'll ignore that. Okay, Chapter Four. We've met. I've
created an excellent impression, it says."

"Wanna bet? You alienated her. I'd be furious if I
were her. First you came on to her in the store, and
then you came on to her friend. Not smart, Mark."

Mark was reading.

You have now created a perfect first impression. Congratulations! Your next step is to solidify it. This is
the most difficult step of all. You must now display
the wit, the charm, the sheer magnetism that is the
embodiment of the successful male. That's you I'm
talking about. Don't look around. I'm talking to
Y-O-U.

"He's talking about me, Toolie. You know, I do feel
successful. I believe in me. How about that?"

"I'd believe in you if you could get my thirty-two
bucks back."

"I will. I will. Anything else I can do for you?"

"Now that you mention it, yes. That girl Rhonda, the
one who was with your Meg, and put that *your* in
quotes, wasn't bad at all. I'd like to meet her."

Mark handed the book to Toolie. "It's all yours. You
can be as successful as me."

"I pass," said Toolie.

"Okay, I'll share it with you. 'Create a plausible reason for seeking her out. But maintain that elusiveness
that she finds so devilishly attractive about you.'"

Mark read it over twice. "Does that mean I should ask her out? How can I do that and be elusive at the same time? Maybe the book will tell me. Be quiet while I concentrate on the next few pages."

"Gladly."

"Ah, here it is in the very next paragraph. 'Do not ask her out on a date. Dates are for dolts. You are more imaginative than that.' "

Mark stared into space. "You know, Toolie, this book is speaking directly to me. I can feel it. It's like I'm exactly the guy it was written for."

"Possibly true. You might be the only person in the country to buy a copy. Remember it was marked down because no one else wanted it."

"You're breaking my concentration. I think this next step is going to do it for me. Meg and I are going to hit it off. This self-confidence thing is wonderful."

"I have confidence that you're going to get my thirty-two bucks back."

Mark closed the book. "I'm all set."

"Exactly what are you going to do? Specifically, exactly."

"I haven't the vaguest idea. But whatever it is, it will work brilliantly."

"Got anything to eat?" asked Toolie. "That Health-burger wasn't very filling."

After Toolie went home, Mark put on his tape cassette and played and replayed some tapes he had made of a song he had written. He wanted to send a tape to Meg Lowman and tell her that he dedicated the song to her. It was so hard to do what he really wanted to do. What if he got rejected? What if she laughed? Sometimes he thought girls liked him. Sometimes he thought they didn't. He felt differently about himself from day to day, sometimes from hour to hour. There were times when he wanted to toss that advice book away. There were moments when he was positive that the advice was not aimed at a talented person like Mark Gardner. If that author really knew him, he might be jealous!

Mark put the book under his bed where he couldn't see it.

9

"Meg, would you answer the door? My hands are full of flour."

"Sure, Mom."

Meg put down the Sunday newspaper. Who was ringing the doorbell at nine o'clock Sunday morning? Her mother was making breakfast and they were both still wearing robes and slippers.

She opened the door.

He was standing there. Mark!

"It's nine o'clock Sunday morning," she said. "And Rhonda doesn't live here. You have the wrong house."

"I have the right house. You live here. I came to see *you*."

Meg liked the way he said *you*. Could he mean it? Maybe she had been right about him at the cosmetics counter.

"I hope I didn't interrupt your breakfast," Mark said.

"How could you? We haven't eaten yet. Do you want to come in?"

She saw that Mark was carrying something. He had a bag from Harriman's Department Store. Could it be a present for her? She pretended she hadn't seen it.

"Who's there?" her mother called.

"A friend of mine," said Meg. Why did she say *that?* Mark smiled.

"The pancakes are ready," her mother called. "Ask your friend if she wants some."

"It's a he." Meg turned to Mark. "Well?"

"I'm crazy about pancakes," said Mark.

"I should have guessed. Come on in the kitchen."

Mrs. Lowman looked up when Meg walked in with Mark. She waited to be introduced.

"Mom, this is Mark Gardner. I know him, uh, from Harriman's. Mark, my mom, Mrs. Lowman."

Mark extended his hand to Meg's mother. She extended a flour-covered one to him.

"Sit down, Mark, put your bag on that chair, and let's eat," she said.

They all sat down. Meg thought the three of them made a strange trio as they sat there eating pancakes. This guy she hardly knew was sitting with her and her mother who were both in their robes and slippers. It looked so domestic. It looked more strange than having Randolph, Charlie, and Burt for lunch. If ten minutes ago someone had told her this scene was about to take place, she would have said it was a total fantasy. But now she had to admit to herself that Mark looked awfully good sitting there at her table. Her mother liked him. She could tell by the way her mother had greeted him. There would be dozens of curious questions afterward. Meg was prepared for that.

"You have marvelous posture, Mark," her mother said suddenly.

"Oh, no," Meg thought. "My mother is big on posture, Mark," she said.

"Well, I guess my confidence shows in the way I sit," he said.

"What are you so confident about?" asked Meg. He was starting to sound conceited.

"It's just that lately someone very knowledgeable has been speaking directly to me, and frankly, making me more aware of, well, where I am in life."

"And where is that?" asked Meg.

"No place special. It's more a way of looking at things." Mark wondered if they could see how hot the back of his neck felt.

"Well, whatever it is, it works," said Mrs. Lowman. "It makes you sit tall. More pancakes?"

"Maybe one more," said Mark.

"Do you live near here?" Meg's mother asked.

Meg knew the questioning was under way, an opportunity her mother couldn't pass up.

"A few miles from here. I go to Portland High. I'll be a junior in the fall."

"How do you and Meg know each other from Harriman's? Coffee?"

Mark squirmed. The back of his neck was definitely heating up! Coffee would make it hotter. But his throat felt dry.

"Yes, please. Well, Mrs. Lowman, it was kind of a merchandise thing."

"Merchandise? Meg works at the cosmetics counter."

Meg almost felt sorry for Mark. He was a better

source of news for her mother than the morning newspaper.

Meg said, "Mark has relatives with all kinds of skin problems. And he likes to give gifts. So that's how he happened to be at my counter.

"How did you know where I live?" Meg asked.

"I knew your last name," Mark explained, "so I looked up Lowman in the telephone directory. There are three. One of the Lowman addresses was on a street near enough to Portland High School so that any high school student living there would have gone to Portland High. But I knew you didn't go to Portland High because I would have noticed you there." Mark's hand hit his coffee cup.

Mrs. Lowman smiled at Meg. This was all sounding good to Mrs. Lowman. Meg sat quietly.

"You really thought this out, didn't you?" said Mrs. Lowman.

"Sure," said Mark. Would they notice that he had spilled some coffee? He felt he was doing very well. The book hadn't even given instructions about finding out where a girl lived. That was certainly an oversight.

He went on. "Well, that left me with two Lowmans. One on William Street and one on Pitt Street. William Street is much nearer to my house, so it seemed to make sense to try the Lowman at William Street first, and, uh, if I was wrong I could walk to the next address, true?"

Mrs. Lowman smiled broadly. Mark felt that she thought she was in the presence of a great mind. Meg must be impressed, too! She was staring at him. This was no time for him to stop. If only the back of his neck wasn't wet!

"It wasn't just that William Street was easier for me to walk to," he continued. "It also is located closer to Harriman's than Pitt Street. I must admit that my reasoning here is a little shaky, but this was an added incentive to try William Street first. And that's about it, and that's why I'm here, and well, here I am!"

Meg and her mother didn't say anything. They were eating silently. "It takes a while to absorb something of such great magnitude," Mark thought as he sipped what was left of his coffee. "I don't think they can see the back of my neck, and they didn't notice the spilled coffee. All they noticed was my—what does the book call it?—sheer magnetism."

Meg was feeling uncomfortable in an ecstatic kind of way. Mark had gone to such trouble to find her! She wished she could go some place for an hour just by herself and think. She would think about him opening the telephone book and finding the three Lowmans and the three different streets they lived on. About how he stared into space while his mind worked feverishly. How his determination to find her was stronger than any obstacle in the way. Some guys would have given up when they saw those three names. Or they would have simply used the telephone and taken a chance of getting a wrong number. That would have been the easy way. But Mark was smart enough to eliminate one Lowman and determined enough to walk right up to the Lowman on William Street and ring the doorbell. Her doorbell. Oh, how she needed to tell him how wonderful that made her feel. She opened her mouth.

"Mom's a cookbook author," she said.

"That's really interesting," said Mark. "Any special foods?"

Mark was thinking, "If she wants to switch the subject to food, that's okay with me. In fact, I approve of it. You can't dazzle people for a long stretch at nine o'clock on a Sunday morning. They're just not prepared for it. Their heads are groggy and their bodies aren't revved up, either."

"Anything and everything," Mrs. Lowman was saying. "I'm on my ninth book."

Mrs. Lowman told Mark about her cookbooks while Meg ate and listened. The three of them were beginning to look like a family sitting in the kitchen. Mark was wearing a blue shirt and his face was slightly flushed. Why not? He had walked all the way over to her house just to see her. By the time breakfast was over, Mark was looking absolutely handsome. "I like him," thought Meg. "Can you fall in love over breakfast?"

When they finished, Mrs. Lowman excused herself to get dressed. Meg and Mark were left at the kitchen table.

"Want to go into the living room?" asked Meg.

"Sure," said Mark. He picked up his bag from the chair and they went into the living room.

Meg wondered, "Is he going to give me a present now?"

As soon as they sat down on the sofa, Mark opened the bag. "I brought these," he said.

Meg felt anxious, excited. No boy had ever given her a present before except when she was a little kid and had birthday parties.

Meg was smiling.

"What a smile," thought Mark. "Am I supposed to ask her for a date? I think she's ready to say yes. But the book says no. Wait. It says I should be elusive at this point. Besides, it says dates are for dolts."

Meg continued to smile.

"I'm just so sure she'd say yes," thought Mark. "But the book was smart enough to get me this far, right into her very own living room. That book knows what it's doing."

Mark pulled out ten tubes of Flaw-Away from the bag.

Meg couldn't believe what she was seeing. Then she thought, "Okay, it's a gag gift. He has a sense of humor."

Mark said, "I was wondering if you could return these for me. I don't have ten relatives with flaws after all."

Mark felt triumphant. He had done it! He had followed the book's instructions exactly. He had worn his best blue shirt even though the book didn't mention clothes in that chapter. He had displayed *wit, charm,* and *magnetism* at the breakfast table. Then he had *created a plausible reason for seeking her out.* He had asked her to return some merchandise. But he would *maintain elusiveness* by not asking her for a date. He was even more clever than the author of the book. Meg would have to see him still *another* time to give him his refund money.

He was looking at Meg. She was gorgeous even on a Sunday morning. Her hair looked uncombed. Her robe was kind of ratty. But she was so fantastic she rose above everything. And now she was looking at him with intensity. Feeling.

She stood up. "Get out!" she said. "Out, out, out!"

"You're kidding, right?"

"Wrong! Out! Go see Rhonda."

"Rhonda. Who's Rhonda?"

"What do you mean who's Rhonda? She's my friend you tried to pick up."

"Oh, that wasn't anything."

"You mean you do it all the time?"

"No, you've got me all wrong."

"Don't forget your merchandise when you leave, which is now."

Meg opened the front door.

"You're slouching," said Mark, as he walked out.

Meg slammed the door behind him.

She glanced at the sofa. Ten tubes of Flaw-Away were scattered over the cushions.

He had forgotten his merchandise.

10

"It wasn't totally successful," Mark said to Toolie.

"What does that mean?" asked Toolie.

"Could have been better," said Mark.

"How much better?"

"Much."

Mark had called Toolie as soon as he got home. It had been a terrible walk home. Four miles of wondering where he went wrong.

"Want me to come over?" asked Toolie.

"Could you?"

"Be right there."

Mark went to his room and pulled *How to Meet a Gorgeous Girl* from his bookcase. Was there perhaps a chapter on errors, goof-ups, disasters? Yes! There it was. Chapter Nine: "If Things Go Wrong—Solace, Remedies, and Ultimate Triumph."

Mark started to read.

The suggestions in this book are not foolproof because, let's face it, guys, what in life is? There are no guarantees. Life is a game to be played wisely. Occasionally we err. The trick is to be resilient. Repeat. Resilient. If you fall, pick yourself up. Got that?

At this point, if you followed my instructions carefully, your gorgeous girl should be ringing your phone constantly, sending you gifts, and in her own way, which differs from girl to girl, showing you that she can't live without you. In the unlikely event that this has not happened to *you*, reflect! You did something wrong. Face it, you *did!*

Mark slammed the book closed and paced around the room. "If I did something wrong, it's because this dumb book told me to. I am finished with this book. I bet the author is some kind of loser. I bet he hasn't had a date in a century. When girls see him coming, they probably cross the street."

Mark kept pacing. "Still, I'm already in trouble. Maybe, at least, the book can tell me how to get out of it. I'll see what it says next. I don't have to do anything about what it says, except maybe laugh. I'll laugh at that guy's ideas. That should make me feel better."

Mark found the place where he had closed the book. He read:

My next piece of advice will shock you. Guys, do nothing. Nothing! You are presently in a state of agitation. Your image—and by Chapter Nine you should have an image or you've really screwed up—

has been severely dented. You are unable to project yourself properly. So don't try. Observe a waiting period—a mourning period if you will—of about two weeks. Two weeks is the statistically proven, optimum cooling-off, winding-down period. Then flex those muscles of yours and get back into action! Got that? Close this book for two weeks.

Mark closed the book as Toolie knocked on his door. "That was fast," Mark said as he opened the door.

"Where are your folks?" asked Toolie.

"In the kitchen. Let's go to my room."

Mark picked up the book. When they got to his room, he closed the door behind them. "I bombed," he said. "I did everything the book said to do including being elusive. Instead of asking Meg for a date, I asked her to return the ten tubes of Flaw-Away."

Toolie groaned. "Say it isn't so."

"It is."

Mark held up the book. "It says if you make a mistake, do nothing for two weeks."

"I can think of something to do," said Toolie. "Throw away the book."

"I'm going to. But I don't have to right now because I'm just going to do nothing for two weeks. I mean, Meg is so mad at me, it will take two weeks just for her to cool off. So I'm not even following the book's advice. I'm just using my own common sense."

Toolie picked up the book and looked at the back flap. "Who is this great dispenser of wisdom, anyway? Dr. Zack Lucifer Hunter. Is that his real name?"

Toolie read:

Dr. Zack Lucifer Hunter, distinguished psychoanalyst and behavioral expert, has written a book
that even the layman can easily understand. In words
that speak directly to the male reader, Dr. Hunter
pulls no punches as he points the way to a more re-
warding, fulfilling life by showing how to meet that
one person you desire. The information in these
pages was previously available only to those who
attended his renowned Hunter Motivation and Behavior Retreat in Gila Bend, Arizona.

Dr. Hunter resides in Pacific Palisades, California.

Toolie put the book down. "I wouldn't have anything
to do with anybody who has anything to do with behavior. *Behavior?* I left that word behind when I was
ten years old."

"It's not that kind of behavior," said Mark. "It's a
grown-up type of behavior. It's sophisticated."

"Okay. Well, like the book says, let it rest for two
weeks, and then go back if you still want to."

"What do you mean, if I still want to? You should
have seen how beautiful she looked this morning. She's
something else."

"So are you. You're not yourself. You're Dr. Hunter's
stooge."

"No, I'm not. And anyway, some of his book is sensi-
ble. Really solid. Dr. Hunter makes sure you can pass
the test before he lets you go out into the world. And I
passed."

"Pass the test? There you go again with words I don't
like."

"It's just a checklist that's in his introduction. Look at

these questions: 'Do you chew gum? Do you wear flashy clothes? Are you clean? Do you slouch? If you can truthfully answer no to the first two questions, yes to question three, and no to question four, you may proceed to Chapter One. If, however, your affirmative answers should have been negative, and your negative answers affirmative, clean up your act—and your body —or nobody will want you!' "

"I've got a test for you," said Toolie. "Are you driving your friend crazy? If you can truthfully answer in the affirmative, clean up your act. Close the book, or your friend will leave."

"Okay. I can wait the two weeks," said Mark. He closed the book and put it in the bookcase. "Let's go into the kitchen and eat breakfast."

"I thought you just ate at Meg's house."

"Yes, but that was a working breakfast. It doesn't count."

11

"Do you have anything for a protruding nose?"

Meg looked up from behind the counter. A woman of about her mother's age was standing there. What was she doing at Young Faces anyway? Meg liked the customers her own age. They came in, sampled everything, giggled, and bought things with a sense of adventure. Then there were the customers like this woman who expected Meg to solve all the problems that age, sun, overindulgence, underindulgence, bad genes, bad luck, and vanity had created.

"Everybody's nose protrudes," said Meg. She hoped that sounded reassuring, and not wise guy.

"Like *mine?*" asked the woman.

Meg's high school offered a course in psychology. Meg was sorry she hadn't taken it. She needed it badly for some of her encounters with customers. She tried not to look at the woman's nose even though a straightforward offer had been extended.

"Well, we do have some products that deemphasize certain features." Meg walked to another part of her counter display. The woman followed on the outside. "Here," said Meg, pointing to little round pots of dark creams that were sitting like colored nests in a sleek white plastic stand. "If you apply one of these sparingly on both sides of your nose and on the tip, it will minimize the size. You can experiment with which of these colors works the best for you. Most customers prefer the brown. It gives a kind of shadowy effect. I'd stay away from the deep pinks. They're popular with some customers, but to me they make the nose reddish, like you've got a cold or something. I'm not supposed to say that, but it's because I really believe in the brown."

The woman said, "Ugh."

"Ugh? You don't like the brown?"

"It's these samples. You can see the fingerprints in them. Look! Squiggly little lines and indentations. I'm not one of these sanitation fanatics, but it seems to me we're looking at a display of germs."

Meg knew the woman had a point. The open samples kept customers from opening fresh containers and testing the contents. But everybody stuck their paws in the samples.

"Well, if you put just a little on the back of your hand you can see how it blends into the skin. Hand sampling isn't as bad as face sampling. I mean, all kinds of junk land up inside your hands. I once saw a documentary called *Journey Through Bacteria* and it told about the life of a penny. You wouldn't believe where that penny had been."

The woman smiled at Meg. "It's all right, dear. I

know you just work here and you're trying to do the best you can. Aren't you young for this job?"

"I guess. It's only for a month."

"Well, you're pretty. I guess that had something to do with hiring you for this counter. Do you go to Portland High?"

"No, Deering High."

The woman looked down at the little pot of creamy brown color. There was a large hollow in it made by countless fingers. She gingerly put her right index finger into it and spread the brown cream on the top of her left hand. She held her hand up to the light. "I just can't tell on my hand," she said.

Meg reached down behind the counter and got a fresh unopened package of Dream Cream. She handed it to the woman. "Here, try it on your nose."

"You're an absolute dear," said the woman. She opened the container eagerly as if it were a prize she had just won. She gazed down at the untouched brown cream. "Ever feast your eyes on pristine beauty?" she said to Meg. "Well, here it is."

The woman put a fresh finger into the brown cream. Then she rubbed the cream on one side of her nose.

"No, like this," said Meg. "Is it okay if I rub your nose?"

"Rub!" The woman leaned eagerly toward Meg.

"She likes attention," Meg thought. "She's one of those women who are proud of being fussed over and analyzed. She likes being an object." Meg tried not to think of the way dogs sit with pride and patience while fleas are extracted from their fur.

Meg skillfully blended the cream on both sides of the

woman's nose. Then she put a touch of it on the tip. "There."

The woman looked in a mirror. She turned her head back and forth to see various angles. Meg looked away. She didn't want to intrude upon the woman's moment of private decision.

"I *think* it's an improvement, don't you?" the woman said finally. She was facing Meg head-on.

"Yes, it works," said Meg. "But you have to be careful to put on just a touch."

"I'll take it," said the woman. "You're a dear. It's refreshing to meet a nice little teen-ager. So many of them spend their summers stealing hubcaps and sleeping in video arcades."

"Cash or charge?"

"Cash."

Meg started to write up the sale.

"Do you go out with college boys?"

Meg looked up. "What?"

"College boys. I have a nephew visiting me. He's a college boy. Very fine young man. He hardly knows anyone in town, and well, I'd like him to have a little social life. Is a college boy too old for you?"

"Well, I hadn't . . ."

"He makes dean's list all the time. And he's not what you girls call a makeout artist. Shaun is really a lovely boy. But not dull. He's interested in hang-gliding."

"I, uh, don't know what to say."

"You're not pinned or anything?"

"Pinned?"

"Well, in my generation if a girl and boy went out exclusively and if he gave her his fraternity pin, they would be what we call pinned."

"I'm not going out with anyone." Meg was trying to write up the sales slip and answer the woman at the same time. Maybe it would be okay to meet this Shaun. She hadn't had a date yet this summer.

"I've put you on the spot, haven't I?" said the woman. "Well, forget I said anything. My husband says I'm a matchmaker and he's probably right. How much do I owe you?"

"Six twenty-five including tax."

"That much? I should have known. The smaller the container, the more it costs." The woman took the money from her pocketbook and handed it to Meg. Meg rang up the sale and put the cream and sales slip in a bag.

Meg handed the woman the bag. "It's a real pleasure to start off my shopping day with someone like you," said the woman, and she left. For the first time, Meg saw her in profile. The woman had been absolutely right about her nose.

12

It was Sunday again. Would the doorbell ring at nine and Mark Gardner be there for another early morning breakfast? What a ridiculous thought! Meg was watching her mother make pancakes. They reminded her of Mark's visit.

It had been a week since Mark Gardner had come by. It had been a week since she had seen him at all. He had stopped coming to her counter. Not a sign of him anywhere. Could there be something about a Sunday morning that would bring him back again? Wouldn't it be great if he came by at eleven this morning. Eleven would be about right. She and her mother would be two miles away at eleven. Mark would ring the bell. He would be very hungry. He would ring and ring. Nobody home. Tough luck, Mark.

Every other Sunday morning Meg and her mother went to pick up Grandma Seeny and bring her back for dinner. Seeny was her grandmother's made-up first name. Her real name was Trish, but she had named her

daughter Trish, and so they became Trish Senior and
Trish Junior. That became confusing, so Grandma was
called simply Senior. But she didn't go for that, so it
was shortened to Seeny. "You'd think she would have
thought of all the problems before she went ahead and
named her very own daughter after herself," Meg told
her mother. "Still, fathers do it all the time with sons.
I'll never name a kid of mine Meg."

At ten thirty Meg and her mother were on their way.
Mark hadn't come.

Grandma Seeny had moved to town about six weeks
ago to be near "my family." Since she had four children
in addition to Meg's mother, that didn't seem quite ac-
curate to Meg. She and her parents were only part of
Seeny's family. But the other four children were boys.
Men. "A daughter," Grandma Seeny kept repeating. "A
daughter, she's close. That's the way it should be.
Close."

Meg didn't think of Grandma Seeny as a granny type,
if there was one. She had been married twice and divorced twice. "I'm not a little widow lady," she was
fond of saying. That sounded terrible to Meg. If
Grandma Seeny had stuck with her husbands long
enough, one of them might have died on her. Grandma
Seeny has nothing to brag about.

Meg wondered why her mother had taken an apartment for Grandma Seeny at Serenity Village. "It's as
boring as it sounds," Meg had told Rhonda. "Actually,
more boring." To Meg, it sounded like a fancy ceme-
tery. But the name was meant to discourage families
with small children. Meg thought the name would discourage anybody.

Serenity Village was located two miles from Meg's house. It was a new apartment complex of five red brick buildings surrounded by large expanses of manicured lawns, trees, and red, white, and blue flower beds. It looked like the product of an orderly, structured mind. There was nothing chancy about Serenity Village.

There was another new apartment complex not far from Serenity Village. It was aimed for "singles." "Grandma belongs in that one," Meg had told her mother before Grandma Seeny moved to town. "Get her an apartment there."

"Not dignified. Loose. Forget it," her mother had answered.

"You'll be sorry," Meg had predicted.

Her mother was. Grandma Seeny hated Serenity Village the minute she saw it. "Why did you sentence me to this geriatric jail?" she asked.

Meg's mother had signed a two-year lease.

"Everyone is entitled to make a mistake," Meg's mother had said, "but I'm going to pay and pay for this one. She hates it there. She'll be over here every day. She'll expect me to pick her up and take her back and I'll go bananas."

"Maybe she'll make some friends her own age," Meg had said.

"Her own age? She doesn't have an age. She loses hundreds of dollars in discounts each year just because she won't admit she's a senior citizen. Not that I blame her. Would you want to be classified as a junior citizen? People can't just get older anymore. One year you're a person, the next year you're a category. You're stuck in

a club with involuntary membership and they stamp
you Fragile—Handle With Care."

"There's nothing fragile about Grandma Seeny. Do
you really think she'll want to hang out here all the
time?"

"You've got it."

"But won't she know that'll be a drag for you?"

"A drag? She'll rationalize that she'll be company for
me since Dad travels so much. And she'll reason, quite
sensibly, that it's only a two-mile drive each way between our places. That couldn't put me out very much.
Just a hop and a skip between us. If I had rented a
place for her miles and miles from here, I'd have an
excuse. I don't want to hurt her feelings, but I have my
own life. And she should cultivate people her own age,
whatever that may be."

"You don't think she'd expect to come over every day
if she lived miles and miles from here?"

"No, but it's too late now. I had to go and sign that
two-year lease. Maybe I can find someone to sublet.
That's a hassle, of course. What do you think?"

"I'm still thinking about miles and miles," Meg said.

Somewhere in that conversation an idea was born.
When Meg looked back, she couldn't remember who
thought of it first. It seemed like a joke, a joke that got
more and more plausible as she and her mother talked.

"If we do it, we have to do it immediately," her
mother had said. "On the very first trip."

"Of course," Meg agreed.

"But it's not a nice thing to do, is it?"

"The end justifies the means," Meg said.

"It won't work," her mother said.

"I bet it will."

And so they did it. Today they would be doing it for the third time, Meg was thinking as they drove into the parking lot at Serenity Village. Instead of driving Grandma Seeny the two miles to their house, which was about a five-minute trip, they would once again take a circuitous route home. They would drive miles and miles around the city. Grandma Seeny was smart. But she had absolutely no sense of direction. There was no such thing as a familiar landmark to her. She never knew where she was on the road. And now she was in a new town which made it even more difficult to get a fix on her location. So she didn't realize that she was being driven almost twenty-five miles out of the way to get to her daughter's house. She thought her daughter *lived* twenty-five miles away. That added up—and Grandma Seeny was good at adding up—to a total of one hundred miles for her daughter to pick her up, drive her to the house, drive her back and drive home. And so Grandma Seeny was satisfied with a trip every other Sunday.

Meg and her mother drove a total of almost fifty miles out of their way every other Sunday, which amounted to less mileage than if the two short round trips were made every day. "It works out economically, too," Meg's mother said. "It's a true gas saver."

Grandma Seeny was ready and waiting for them. She was dressed in a pink tunic and pants. Her blond hair was tucked under a large white hat that had a wide pink band around it. She was wearing high-heeled black sandals. Meg thought her grandmother looked particularly happy. A day with the family must be a real upper for her, she thought, and Meg suddenly felt guilty. Grandma Seeny beckoned them in.

There was a man inside! Meg wondered if this accounted for Grandma Seeny's great mood. The man looked about Grandma Seeny's age. That was the go-figure-it-out age. He was wearing a print shirt and white pants, and he had a tan. He looked like one of those prosperous men who are forever on vacation and have just cleaned up after a brisk swim in a pool. He smiled and extended his hand.

"Trish, Meg," said Grandma Seeny, "I want you to meet my friend August Knotts. August recently sold his nail factory."

Grandma Seeny had a new male friend! Hallelujah! Meg saw her mother grasp August Knotts's hand like a sinking person grabs a rescuer. Was she afraid he would get away? "I can't tell you how happy I am to meet you," she said.

"If she tells him," Meg was thinking, "he'll flee. He's going to be husband number three, I just know it. It's easier for Grandma to get a boyfriend than it is for me. Maybe when I'm a grandmother I'll do terrific."

"August lives just above me," said Grandma Seeny. "One night I was playing my stereo too loud and he came down to complain."

"Best complaining I ever did," August Knotts chuckled.

Meg and her mother exchanged looks. Grandma Seeny had met her *second* husband by playing her *radio* too loud! She had moved into a new apartment house after she divorced her first husband. She knew no one. She had reasoned that a blasting radio would attract the people next door on both sides, across the hall, directly over her and directly under her. From all those possibilities, there might be "someone interesting" to meet. She had nothing to lose. "It's infinitely easier than packing up and going on a cruise," she had explained to Meg's mother. So she did it one Sunday afternoon. From three doors away had come her future husband number two, disturbed from his nap, resolutely and innocently shuffling down the hall in his pajamas and slippers to his destiny of a three-year marriage with the enterprising blond occupant of apartment 5C.

"I hope you don't mind, but I invited Augie to have dinner with us at your house," said Grandma Seeny.

"I'm just delighted," said Meg's mother.

"I hope it's not an imposition," said August Knotts. "It's been a long time since I've been to dinner at a private home in this city. I grew up here and moved away. When I came back, I moved straight into Serenity Village."

"Oh, then you know our city?" Meg asked him while looking directly at her mother.

"Like the back of my hand," said August Knotts. "Do you live far from here?"

"Yes and no," said Meg's mother.

"Oh, it's such an interesting ride to their house," said Grandma Seeny. "We go past all these shopping malls and parks and houses and more houses and more parks and things. I tell you there's so much to see, it gets confusing. It's hard to know where you are in this city."

"Actually it's quite easy," said August Knotts. "The city is laid out in a grid pattern. Most of the streets are parallel with or at right angles to one another. The city looks like graph paper. I can teach the layout to you in five minutes tops."

Meg's mother spoke up. "I don't know how to say this without seeming impolite, but I suddenly remembered that I scraped together a few leftovers for dinner today. I hardly have enough for three people, let alone four."

Meg knew this was true. Although being true was beside the point.

"I understand perfectly," said August Knotts. "The fact is that it would be my pleasure to take all of you out to dinner. I won't take no for an answer."

"Well, then, we accept," said Meg's mother. "And we hope to have you at our house real soon."

Meg knew that her mother would enjoy this dinner. She had indefinitely postponed August Knotts's trip to her house! "Real soon" would be translated into delays, procrastination, excuses, weeks, months, years, infinity. Seasons would change, the earth would orbit around and around the sun, and still an invitation would not be forthcoming.

But today was too pleasant to think about that. Meg was glad to be going out to eat. She was glad to be away from her house for the day. If Mark came by, he might hang around waiting and waiting, thinking she could come back any minute. On this beautiful Sunday she was keeping him waiting. She liked doing that, even though she knew it was only in her head.

13

"Hi. I'm Shaun."

Meg looked up from rearranging a lotion display.

Someone was standing at her counter. He was wearing a blazer. He looked crisp and tailored. He was a stranger.

"Shaun? That's nice. Can I help you with something?"

"My aunt Margaret told me to stop by and introduce myself."

"Your aunt Margaret? Oh, yes." Meg now remembered. The woman with the monumental nose. "Well, hi."

"Hi."

"You're the nephew who's visiting her?"

"Yes. And she suggested that I might want to meet you. Get to know you."

Meg didn't know how to reply. This guy with his short hair and piercing eyes reminded her of a recruitment poster for a military academy.

"How about lunch?" he asked.

Lunch? If she went to lunch with him she would miss today's installment of *Tomorrow's Yesterday*. Not that she watched it every day. But in a vague kind of way she was looking forward to seeing Rick. What a silly reason for turning down an invitation to lunch with this guy! He seemed respectable and safe, the way boys are that you meet through their aunts or mothers.

"Okay," she said. "I get off at noon."

"Then I'll meet you here at noon. I thought we'd go to Michelle's Corner."

"Michelle's Corner? Fine." Meg tried to be casual. Michelle's Corner was the most expensive restaurant in the mall. She had never been inside. It seemed to be a place for executives and rich shoppers. She wondered if anyone under thirty had ever set foot inside, except for the help.

"See you then," said Shaun.

"See you then."

Meg supposed that Dream Cream had worked out very well on Aunt Margaret's nose. "Well, it's the first sign of life at this counter since Mark Gardner stopped coming around," she thought. "But Mark Gardner is past history. And Shaun is at noon."

At exactly twelve Shaun was back. Mrs. Cogshell came around at the same time, so Meg got her purse and left with Shaun.

Shaun was a fast walker. Meg found it hard to keep up with him as they walked down the mall.

"I've made a reservation for us," he said.

Meg had never been out with a guy who made reservations.

"Good idea," she said.

Michelle's Corner was at the far end of the mall. They passed a line waiting at Beefy Burg. "Vile stuff," said Shaun. "Why would anyone stand in line for it?"

"Some people have no taste," said Meg.

Why did she say that? She wasn't above Beefy Burg. It was just about at her level. There were no lines outside Michelle's Corner. Inside it was dark and leathery looking, like a private club. Meg had never been in a private club, but she had seen men sitting around in them in cigar ads. Meg wondered what a restaurant like this was doing in a shopping mall.

"Reservations for two for Chadsworth," said Shaun.

"So that's his last name," thought Meg. "Now I've got a full name for him. But he doesn't know mine. Or does he? He seems to have a way of accomplishing things, of taking over, of *knowing*."

"Tell me about yourself," he said after they had been seated and had given their orders. Meg had ordered something which was medium-priced for the menu but high-priced for her.

"My name is Meg Lowman and I'm a high school student."

"What's your ambition?"

"My ambition?"

"Most girls have ambitions these days. You girls have been downtrodden too long. I'm all for your breaking out."

"I'm working on it. What about you? What are you studying in college?"

Meg sensed he had been waiting to be asked. Sometimes guys asked questions they wanted to answer themselves.

"Premed. I'm going to be a doctor. I'll also be studying business management."

"Both?"

"Well, one can hardly be a doctor in our current eco-
nomic climate without having business expertise."

"One couldn't?" Meg wanted to kick herself. She
hadn't meant to mock him. But he didn't notice.

"Look, healing is going to be my big thing. The old-
fashioned concept of the dedicated physician is something that I personally am going to nourish and pro-
mote. I hope to treat the *truly* sick, not the marginally
sick or the imaginary sick."

"How can you tell in advance?"

"There are types. The ones who don't carry medical
insurance, the ones who won't agree to a credit check,
they come to you with a splinter because they have no
intention of paying. A doctor can't spread himself thin.
Lost medical productivity is inexcusable."

Meg had a vision of sick people standing in a line
longer than Beefy Burg's at noon. And there was Dr.
Shaun with his stethoscope around his neck and his
ledger in his hands interviewing them before they were
allowed to enter his hallowed office. A few of them
collapse on the sidewalk. Dr. Shaun is careful when he
steps over them.

Their order came. While she was eating, Meg decided she was being unfair to Shaun. "We all have our
little blind spots," she thought. "By the time he gradu-
ates from medical school he might have turned into the
kindly physician who makes house calls and eats
homemade cookies and forgets to send a bill."

Her thoughts were interrupted by Shaun.

"Now there's an example of productivity waste," he

said. "Our waitress is gossiping with another waitress. Look at that." Shaun nodded to his left. "Customers are probably waiting for them, food in the kitchen is getting cold or overheated . . ."

Meg was beginning to feel sorry for Shaun. How old was he anyway? Nineteen or fifty? He was rigid and dogmatic, not in the way some of her superidealistic friends were, but in a settled, establishment kind of way that she thought was supposed to hit a person about the same time as middle-age paunch.

"Seen any good movies lately?" She tried to steer him to a fun topic.

"Yes. *Pervert at the Party*. Excellent."

Meg laughed. "I'll bet."

"I'm serious."

"Serious? That's an X-rated film. I heard it was, well, perverted."

"Some parts of it were. But most movies are mindless pap with obvious messages. The X-rated ones have subliminal messages, if you're alert to them. They're a challenge."

"I wouldn't have thought that a guy like you would like dirty movies."

"Now there you go prejudging. If you think of them as dirty, they will be. But if you open your mind to them, they're not. It's so trendy to say 'Oh, I wouldn't see *that*,' but how do you know about *that* unless you've seen it?"

"I hadn't really thought about it that way."

"Exactly my point."

Meg was thinking, of course there had to be a point to everything. She decided to concentrate on her herb-fried chicken. Shaun was enjoying his trout in wine sauce.

He looked up. "What do you think of my aunt?"

"Nice lady."

"You met her through her nose, didn't you? At the cosmetics counter. She could only have been there for one thing. She takes great pride in that nose."

"That's not the impression I got. I thought it bothered her."

"Believe me, it doesn't. It's something of consequence, don't you see? She wasn't stamped out from the same cookie cutter as everyone else. What you got was a surface impression of my aunt. Unfortunately most of us simply flit through life with our surface impressions. We don't take the time to look underneath. We don't care enough."

"I agree with you there."

"Are you a person who cares?"

"What do you mean?"

"I mean do you bother to go through all that getting acquainted nonsense, that 'I don't know you well enough' nonsense, all that rot before you show a guy how much you care?"

For the first time, Meg felt she understood Shaun's point. She wasn't quite sure how he had gotten to that point. He was more clever than any other boy she had been out with. Then again, she had never been out with a snake. Shaun had sort of slithered smoothly along until suddenly he struck. At high noon. Over his trout in wine sauce. Actually it was past high noon. High noon was when Shaun had begun his scheme. Meg realized that he knew all along what he was after. She glanced down at her watch. It was quarter to one. It had taken him three quarters of an hour to make his move. Not record time. Guys in cars sometimes become obvious in two seconds flat.

Meg wanted to get up and leave. But it might cause a scene. It was easier to stay and end the lunch pleasantly.

"Well?" He was waiting.

"I don't believe in that nonsense either. My boyfriend, uh, Mark, and I—well, neither of us believe in that nonsense."

"You have a boyfriend?"

"Didn't your aunt tell you?"

Meg didn't feel dishonest saying that. After all, Auntie hadn't told her the most important thing about Shaun.

"Is he your favorite boyfriend?"

"He's my only boyfriend. Childhood sweethearts, you know. Lived next door to each other, all of that."

"Does he know you're out with another guy?"

"Out with? Gee, I never thought about it that way. It's lunch in broad daylight. Sometimes I eat with strangers in a cafeteria."

"Do you have any free girlfriends?"

"Nobody I dislike enough to fix up with you," Meg thought. This guy was unreal. He hadn't given the possibility of a relationship with her a decent burial before he went on to another candidate.

"They're not your type," said Meg.

"What does that mean?"

"It wouldn't work out."

"I see."

Now *he* was interested in ending the lunch.

He paid the check, and then they said good-bye just outside the door of Michelle's Corner. He didn't offer to take Meg home.

Meg strolled down the mall by herself, watching the crowds, gazing into windows, stopping at displays of crafts and artwork that were set up among the plants and benches and fountains. It felt cleansing.

She talked with some of the artists who were sitting next to their paintings. She would have bought something if she had had enough money. It was hard to make a living as an artist. It must be something like writing your ninth cookbook and hoping to get it published.

She walked on. Why had she said she had a boyfriend named Mark? She knew why. Because she liked Mark Gardner. Being with Shaun made her realize how much. She didn't know why Mark did the things he did, but she wanted to look beyond them. There was a real Mark out there she wanted to know.

But what could she do about it?

14

Meg sat at her desk and wrote, "Dear Cousin Shari." Then she put down her pen.

Meg hated writing letters. When she was a child she was taught that she was supposed to ask *how are you* and then she was supposed to write *I am fine.* But what if she wasn't fine? Nobody had told her what to write if she had a problem.

She hadn't actually seen her cousin Shari Stapleton in almost two years. They lived in different cities. But Meg often thought of Shari—they were about the same age, and the last time they were together they talked as if they were best friends. Meg didn't feel she could turn to Rhonda. Maybe someone who wasn't involved would help. Meg picked up her pen again. She crossed out the word *Cousin.* Too formal. Then she wrote,

Surprise! I know you didn't expect this letter. I'm sorry that it's been a year and a half since I wrote to you, but I hate to write letters. Don't you? Well, anyway, I hope you don't hate it enough to keep from answering this. I need advice. My best friend, Rhonda Schwartz, has plenty, but she is so close to my situation that she could be missing something that you, far away, could see. Does that make sense? Please think about it and it will make sense.

Now you're wondering what my situation is. Well, there's a guy I met at my job (I'm working behind a cosmetics counter in a department store) and his name is Mark and he kind of comes and goes in my life. What do you think about a guy who pays a lot of attention to you and then he doesn't? And just when you think he likes you, he does something to make you think he doesn't. So what do you think about this?

I hope you're not having any problems, but if you are, please tell me about them because I'm far away and I might have some perspective.

Love to your mom and Milton.

Love,
Meg

P.S. I'm desperate. *Please* answer.

Meg decided to wait a day until she mailed the letter. Maybe tomorrow she'd change her mind about telling someone something personal about herself. Maybe tomorrow the letter would seem stupid. But then she counted the days it might take for the letter to reach Shari and for an answer to come back. If she was going to send the letter, she should just go and do it. Meg went to the mailbox.

She was thrilled when a letter came from Shari but not surprised. "I knew she'd come through," Meg smiled as she opened the envelope.

Dear Meg,

It was great hearing from you!! We're both lucky. I've learned plenty about boys since the last time I saw you. I have a boyfriend now. His name is Craig— Craig Andrew—nice name, huh? I met him when he was a senior. It's a long story. He graduated from high school in June and he's going to start college right here in town in the fall. The big thing about guys is to realize that they might be trying to understand *you*. If a guy is a puzzle to you, you could be a puzzle to him. So my advice is to be polite to this guy Mark and just wait and see what happens next. Pretty soon you'll find out what's on his mind.

Please write and let me know what happens. I'll send you a picture of Craig and me just as soon as I get a good one.

Love to your parents. How's grandma? Do you see her often? *Write soon.*

Lots of love,
Shari

Meg was glad she had written to Shari. She promised herself she'd be a better letter writer and answer soon. It did make sense to wait and see what happened with

Mark. And being furious at him certainly hadn't gotten her anywhere.

Whenever she had an unfriendly thought about Mark, Meg reread Shari's letter. And she dreamed about sending a picture of herself and Mark to Shari.

15

"I've got a job," Mark Gardner said to Toolie as they jogged around the high school track early one morning. "Two days a week. I'm practically a business tycoon."

"It's better than no days a week," said Toolie. "How did it happen? I mean, one minute you're unemployed, and the next minute you're making money, money, money. Don't mind me. My envy is showing. So where are you tycooning?"

"The money is minimum wage," said Mark. "And I got the job because I'm at the Record Time store in the mall so much. They know me there. They know I'm knowledgeable about music. Well, actually, they found out I'm a musician, too. We rap a lot. Then this opening came up. It's not exactly an opening. It's more like their summer employee schedule is a little crazy because of vacations and days off, and they asked me to fill in the cracks. Two days a week."

"What days?"

"That's the catch. They're not necessarily the same days each week. They tell me what days to come in, and sometimes they'll tell me at the very last minute."

"That's no way to treat a business tycoon," said Toolie, as they sat down to rest.

"It gets a little better," said Mark. "There's only a few weeks left before school starts. Then they're letting me work Saturdays. At least some Saturdays."

Toolie took off his sneaker and shook out some pebbles. "Did they perhaps reveal to you the day when you're supposed to show up to work for the first time?"

"Today."

"And you're *here?*"

"All I have to do is run home, take a shower, dress, catch a bus to the mall, and I'm all set. You know, I bet it'll feel strange arriving at the mall before anything is open. It's like being an insider or something."

"Maybe I'll be an insider at Beefy Burg some day," said Toolie.

"Don't give up hope," said Mark. "Look, I got a job. Maybe you should try in a store where you have some kind of expert knowledge."

"I have expert knowledge about Beefy Burgs," said Toolie. "I know they're made of sawdust and recycled chewing gum."

"You've got it made," said Mark. "Well, I've got to run. Run home."

"Good luck on your first day. Seriously," said Toolie. "I'm going back on the track and run off my frustration."

An hour and a half later, Mark was on a bus headed for the mall. He was dressed neatly for work.

He was riding with other people who were also dressed neatly for work. It seemed odd to be one of them. It seemed odd to be on the bus so early in the morning. Most of the riders said hello to the driver when they got on the bus. The driver knew them. They knew the driver. It was like a little club. Mark thought it was a nice way to start the day. Being acknowledged early in the morning was like a salute to your existence.

"Hello, Meg."

Mark heard the bus driver's words and saw *her* at the same time. Meg Lowman was getting on the bus! She put her money in the coin box and started to walk down the aisle. She was looking for a seat. There were a few empty seats. One of them was beside Mark.

It seemed to Mark that it would be a good time to hide his head. But he didn't. He looked straight at Meg.

She saw him. She recognized him.

Mark knew she would pass and take an empty seat farther back. She didn't. She stood there and hesitated.

Then she sat down beside Mark.

"Hi," she said.

"Well, hi," said Mark.

"What are you doing on this bus?" she asked.

"Going to work."

"Where?"

"The mall."

"Where in the mall?"

"At Record Time. I'm starting today."

"That's great."

Mark was confused. She seemed friendly. Was she hoping he'd explain what happened that Sunday? She wasn't furious or anything, that was for sure. The book

was right about cooling off. But the two weeks weren't
up yet. Maybe she forgot about that Sunday. Fat
chance. But why should he bring up anything unpleasant? Maybe this was his opportunity, arranged by fate,
arranged by the bus line, arranged by Record Time, to
ask her for a date. He would lead up to it subtly.

"So, how're you doing?" he asked. "Do you always
take this bus?"

"When my mom doesn't drive me."

"How's it going at work?"

"Okay."

"Well, I'll soon find out how it is at work when I start
in the music store. Do you like music? You look like
you'd like music. I'm kind of a musician. The guitar."

"I love guitar music," said Meg.

There wasn't anything Mark wanted to hear more
than that. They had something in common. As the bus
lurched along, stopping and starting, Mark glanced out
his window, which was smeared and had a long crack
near the edge. "This is a beautiful ride," he thought.
"And everything is going to work out. I'm going to ask
her to a concert. A real date. I'll call for her at her
house and take her out. Mark Gardner and Meg Lowman will go out together. Now all I need is a concert to
invite her to. There are groups coming to town all the
time. I'll pick the best one. Maybe some of the guys at
Record Time will have an idea. I'll call Meg tonight."

Meg was looking at Mark. Why was he staring out
the window? Was he going to ask her out? She would
say yes. She wanted to go out with him. She wanted to
ride and ride and ride on the bus with him right now
and just talk. Maybe it was hard to ask a girl out. She

wouldn't want to ask a boy out. Some of her girlfriends did. They said, "Everything is equal now. He can ask you, you can ask him."

The bus stopped. They were at the mall. "We're here," said Mark. They got up and left the bus.

"Well, I have to go to the other end," said Mark. "But I'll be talking to you, I really will."

He walked away.

"He wants to ask me out," Meg told herself. "So why doesn't he?"

When Meg got home after work, she called Rhonda. Since hearing from Shari she no longer felt as dependent on Rhonda as she once did, but there was something up front about Rhonda that Meg needed. Rhonda never fudged.

"Mark Gardner is going to ask me out," Meg said.

"Well, of course he is," said Rhonda. "I keep telling you that he was trying to ask you out that Sunday. The cosmetics stuff was just an excuse to see you. But how come you've become so all-knowing?"

"I saw him on the bus today. He asked me if I liked music. It was a kind of building-up-to-something question."

"And did it?"

"Not yet. But he said he'll be talking to me. He said he really will. He meant it. He was so normal today. It was wonderful."

"So now you believe me. Listen, I'm going to make the most terrific anthropologist. I know just where people are coming from."

"Ha ha and good-bye. I'm going to have lunch."

"So long, newly omniscient friend."

When Meg hung up, she realized she wasn't hungry. She felt like talking and talking. She dialed Grandma Seeny's number.

"Hello." The voice on the other end was alive with enthusiasm.

"Hi, Grandma."

"Meg! How are you, dear?"

"Terrific."

"Go on."

"Go on?"

"Yes. You can't just leave it at that. Is there something new in your young life? Is it a boyfriend? Is he nice?"

"How did you know it's a boy? Never mind, it is. And he *is* nice and he's going to ask me out. He hasn't yet, but he will."

"Listen, dear, men are shy. How do you think I got to know your grandfather? I asked *him* out. That was a shocking thing to do back then. But you do what you have to do."

"Well, I'm just going to wait. So, let's not talk about me anymore. How are you?"

"Augie's coming by any minute. We've joined a committee here. We're going to liven things up. Are you familiar with the isolation factor?"

"Not exactly."

"Good. It's not something you should know about. I'll explain it sometime. Let's just say that Augie and I are going to make Serenity Village less serene. Well, I have to finish getting dressed, but listen—take care of that boyfriend of yours. Don't let anyone snatch him away from you. It's a competitive world, you know."

"Okay, Grandma. Regards to Augie."

After Meg hung up she thought about Grandma Seeny's words. "That boyfriend of yours." It sounded good. A little premature, but good. Mark Gardner would be her boyfriend. It was only a matter of time.

Meg went to her room and wrote a letter to Shari. She was eager to give her an update. Things were looking much better.

16

"I could kick myself!"

Mark Gardner was looking through the entertainment section of the newspaper. "There isn't a decent concert on the horizon. Just a bunch of weird groups coming to town. Meg would hate them."

Mark took out his guitar and started to play. He liked to unwind by playing something with a fast beat. His parents called it "frantic music." Sometimes he thought they disapproved of his guitar playing. They didn't know how much it meant to him.

"Movies," he thought. "I'll ask Meg to the movies." Mark put down his guitar and picked up the newspaper again. He read all the movie listings. None of the movies appealed to him.

Mark started to read the news. "I could take her to a South American rebellion, a congressional hearing, a zoning debate. Here's a good one. The grand opening of a supermarket." Mark threw the newspaper to the floor.

"It's not the concerts or the movies. It's me. I've lost my guts. I should have asked her right there on the bus when I had the chance. I bet I looked dumb to her just sitting there. If she could see me now in my natural setting with my guitar, and my talent, well, she'd really be impressed. But sitting there on that old bus beside a smeared and cracked window, it just wasn't the real Mark Gardner. It's too bad people can't audition for their everyday life like they do for musical shows. I could get up before Meg Lowman and in fifteen minutes she'd see the best of me."

Mark started to play his guitar again. "I've lost my chance. I don't feel it anymore. I had one moment on that bus when I could have asked her out. I even had a chance after we got off the bus. But it's all gone now."

Mark put his guitar away. He reached under his bed and pulled out *How to Meet a Gorgeous Girl*. "Maybe this book knows me better than I know myself. So what if the author is a little off the wall? He's assertive and strong and that's just what I'm not."

Mark opened the book. "Tell me what to do next, book," he said.

17

"Can you get the phone?" Mrs. Lowman called to Meg.

"Sure," said Meg.

For almost a week Meg had been answering the telephone with a sense of anticipation. It could be Mark Gardner calling. But today, finally, she was facing facts. Mark hadn't called. Mark wouldn't be calling. She began to feel angry at him all over again. It was just over two weeks since that Sunday morning when he came over and unloaded his ten tubes of Flaw-Away. And now she was stuck with them. That was another thing. They belonged to him. She couldn't throw them away. And she certainly wasn't going to his house, wherever it was, to return them. She wasn't going to Record Time either. He hadn't mentioned them that day on the bus, so she kept quiet. She almost expected to see him appear at her counter some day, but he hadn't shown up again. Her last day of work was the day after tomorrow. Time was running out for Mark Gardner and his ten tubes of Flaw-Away.

Meg picked up the receiver. "Hello."

"Is this the Trish Lowman residence?" It was a female voice, clipped-sounding.

"Yes."

"Is Mrs. Lowman there?"

"Yes."

"I have Mr. Goodwin on the line for her."

"Just a moment," said Meg. She put down the receiver and went to her mother. "It's a Mr. Goodwin. He wants you," she said.

"Mr. Goodwin? I don't know any Mr. Goodwin. Probably a solicitation. We don't want solar heating, and that's final. They never give up."

Mrs. Lowman picked up the receiver. "Hello."

After that there was a succession of short answers. "Yes, this is she. Yes, I am. Yes, I did."

Then Meg saw her mother's face take on a look of shock. Of joy. Of maniacal madness. The look did not belong in this world. It belonged to a world of surrealistic dreams and impossible events. It belonged to being pursued by elves while your feet stuck to the ground. It belonged to falling off a skyscraper and landing sitting under a palm tree. It belonged to getting a cookbook published!

Meg felt her mother's joy. It was her joy, too. It was a victory built on eight defeats. Never give up. It was corny. Sometimes it was true.

Meg tried to pick up details from her mother's end of the conversation. But it was jumbled. When she hung up, her mother would tell her everything. Ten times over. Her mother would float around in her own sphere. Meg could even slouch unnoticed, unchastised.

Her mother was on the telephone about fifteen minutes. When the conversation was over, she grabbed Meg and hugged her like a rag doll. "It's getting published!" she cried. "I can't believe it. Oh, I have to call your father. Where's his number?"

"What time is it in Japan, Mom?"

"I don't know. Your father told me about the time difference, but I can't think straight. I don't care if it's midnight there. He'll be glad to be waked up for news like this."

"His number is on the bulletin board," said Meg. "The green piece of paper, remember?"

"Oh, yes," said Mrs. Lowman, and she sat down.

"Okay, you just get yourself together and I'll dial the call," said Meg.

Meg took the paper from the bulletin board. "Boy, this is some number."

"Well, there's an international access code and a country code and a routing code and a local telephone number," said Mrs. Lowman. "Or something like that."

"And it all works?"

"Usually," said Mrs. Lowman. "Not that I've really used it that much. Actually I've only called your father twice. But the number is nice to have around. Like a security blanket."

"I'll just dial and see what happens," said Meg. Meg dialed all the numbers carefully and waited. "I don't think anything is happening," she said.

"Give it time," said her mother.

"Hello," said Meg. "Hello. Who is this? What? No, I said who is this?"

"What's happening?" asked her mother.

"I can't make it out," said Meg. She spoke into the receiver. "Do you speak English? *English.*"

Meg waited. The person on the other end spoke again. She sounded as if she knew what she was talking about. But she was speaking in a foreign language. "This is ridiculous," thought Meg. "This is like talking to Mark Gardner. A lot of words but no communication. Not that I've ever spoken to Mark on the phone. Not that I ever *will!*"

She turned to her mother. "I'll have to hang up," she said. "I can't understand the person on the other end and she can't understand me. And this noncommunication is probably costing a fortune."

"I'll try tomorrow," said Mrs. Lowman. "Anyway, let me tell *you* everything. There's so much to tell."

Meg hung up. She sat down beside her mother.

Mrs. Lowman grabbed Meg's hand. "Well, Meg, basically they—Preston House Press—*love* my cookbook. They've already tested some of the recipes, but what makes my book special, he said, is its humanity. Get that? Humanity in a cookbook. The idea of the five diners, what I wrote in the preface, just wowed them. They haven't had the manuscript long, either. Mr. Goodwin said there was immediate enthusiasm—I think those were his words. He's not using all the recipes. He said something about using half or one third or something, and it's going to be paperback because that sells the most copies and it's going to have a picture of the five diners on the cover. Usually they just have pictures of food or pots and pans or just the title. But he said the picture of the five real diners would define the book's distinctiveness. I remember those words exactly."

"Oh, what fun! I wonder what recipes they'll choose. And how much money you'll get."

"Wait, wait, wait," said Mrs. Lowman. "One thing at a time. I have approval over what recipes they use. In other words, if I feel strongly that I'd like something in that they want out, I have the final say. They want a balanced group of dishes. And they're writing me about contract terms. A *contract!* Savor the sound of *that.* And they're getting a photographer to do the cover. Somebody experienced in covers."

"Whoa! A photographer?"

"Yes. It's all so incredible." Meg's mother bent down and kissed a mixing spoon that was on the kitchen table. "Mmmm. I love you!"

Meg didn't want to say anything that would dim her mother's happiness. It would sink in soon enough that a photographer would be coming around to take a picture of Randolph, Charlie, Burt, and one other dilapidated diner. The retired judge, the two men on sabbatical from the biophysical science field, and the wine-tasting expert would be gracing the cover of a book that was supposed to whet the readers' appetites.

Then Meg had another thought. "Models! They'll use models. Not real people. Representation. Misrepresentation. The last thing the public wants to see is people who look like regular people. That's a real downer. I can just imagine who the publisher will get for the cover of Mom's book. The judge. He'll have silver hair and one of those silver moustaches that curl up. Maybe they'll picture him in his judicial robes. Like saying that Mom's recipes are so good, he sat down and tried them between trying cases. The two scientists.

They could have test tubes sticking out of their immaculate white coats. They'll look extremely intellectual and have receding foreheads. And the wine taster. Probably a woman because otherwise the cover will be sexist. She'll be elegant. She'll make Ms. Selwyn look like she came from the city dump. Silver hair, like the judge's. It will be swept back, and she'll be wearing a silk dress with a string of pearls. She'll be holding a sparkling glass with one of those thin stems and it will have sparkling red liquid in it."

"Oh no! They're going to come and take Randolph's and Charlie's and Burt's pictures. And the fourth wino, whoever it is. I'm ruined!" Mrs. Lowman was screaming.

"Mom, take it easy."

"It didn't register while I was talking to Mr. Goodwin. But he said, and I remember it clearly now, that a photographer would be sent to take a picture of the five diners eating lunch here." Mrs. Lowman swept her hand across her forehead wearily. "What am I going to do? How am I ever going to get those guys cleaned up and looking presentable? And how do I keep the photographer from falling over from the smell of muscatel and Kitty Litter?"

Mrs. Lowman got up and walked around the room. "Do you suppose your father would mind if we borrowed some of his clothes?"

"Randolph's kind of fat. He's got that big front."

"We could keep the suit jacket open."

"Dad's suits? I thought you meant a shirt or something. Maybe the bottom half of what they're wearing won't show in the picture. If the top half of them looks okay, then you're home free."

"But the photographer might carry tales back to the publisher. And what about the things that can't be seen, but are there? Like, do you suppose Dad's cologne would cover the Kitty Litter smell?"

"Air freshener will. Just spray the room before they come instead of after they leave like you usually do."

"Won't that hurt their feelings?"

"They'll probably be too excited to notice."

"You think so? Is this going to work? I mean, this 'event'?"

"Sure. All we have to do is make a list of our problems and then we match it up with a list of solutions."

"Meg, you're terrific. I'm beginning to think we can pull this off together. I'll never mention slouching to you again. With a head like yours, you can get anybody."

"Ten tubes of Flaw-Away say I can't," thought Meg.

18

"My two weeks are more than up," Mark said to Toolie. They were walking in the mall.

"What willpower," said Toolie. "You survived over two weeks without that book. Talk about self-deprivation."

"I don't *need* that book, but you can't knock what it says next."

"Which is?"

"Well, it's a free-flow section."

"Free flow? What's that?"

"It means, go with the flow. The new chapter is all about instinct. And spontaneity. You just go with whatever hits you at the moment!"

"What if nothing hits?"

"It will. If I let it. That's the point. The book says I should be weaning myself away from the book at this point. I should become my own person, free and spontaneous."

"That's what I've been telling you. And you didn't

pay me two dollars and ninety-five cents for the advice either. In fact, your gorgeous-girl insanity cost me over thirty bucks and you still owe it to me."

"I just have to get the Flaw-Away stuff back, and then I can get your money back."

"How? When?"

"I'm working on it in my head."

"I'm not impressed by your working area."

Suddenly Toolie turned around. He walked toward the entrance of Harriman's Department Store.

"Wait!" called Mark. "What are you doing?"

But Toolie didn't stop. He went into the store and marched up to the cosmetics counter where Meg was talking with a customer. When she was through, she turned to him. "May I help you with something?"

"Well, yes," said Toolie. "I don't know how to say this, but you've got ten tubes of Flaw-Away that belong to me."

"To you?"

"Yuh. Maybe you remember me. I was in line at Beefy Burg with Mark Gardner when you were with your friend. And Mark went up to your friend. Well, anyway, he bought the Flaw-Away with my money."

"Your money? I don't get it."

"Well, I've told you more than I should, but I really need the money. So if you could just return the stuff to the store and get my refund for me, I'd appreciate it a lot. I'm risking my life just standing here because if that snooty lady sees me again she could make trouble for me. And Mark is probably mad at me because I'm here. I can feel his eyes burning through the back of my head."

"Mark? Where is he?"

"Look over at the shoe department. I don't want to turn my head. Is he there?"

"Yeah, now I see him. I mean it looks like him from here, but I'm not sure. He put you up to this, didn't he? To get *his* money back?"

"No. Honestly. I lent him the money. He'll never buy anything else from you and I won't return anything else. But just this once, please do it. You do have the stuff, don't you? You didn't throw it away?"

"It's at home," said Meg. "Okay, okay. It's just cluttering up my dresser anyway. I didn't know what to do with it. I'll *try* to return it. No promises. I'll write up the return, but Ms. Selwyn is an ogre, and she says she is watching my performance. She can't watch much longer. Tomorrow is my last day here so she can't fire me. But I'd like a good reference from her. I hope this doesn't wreck it."

"You're a good sport," said Toolie. "One last thing, where do I get my money? I don't want to show my face here again."

"How about tomorrow at twelve fifteen at Beefy Burg?" said Meg.

"Will you be with your friend?" asked Toolie.

"Rhonda? Maybe. We have lunch together sometimes."

"Hey, can you introduce me to her?"

"Your pal Mark's interested in her."

"You mean you didn't see through that?"

"See through what?"

"Figure it out. Well, I gotta go. Remember the two *R*s. Refund and Rhonda, okay?"

"I think I'm being snowed. But okay."

Meg watched Toolie walk off. She saw Mark join him. Mark grabbed Toolie by the shoulder. Was he mad at Toolie? Maybe Toolie was telling the truth about the money. And maybe Toolie really wanted to meet Rhonda. Meg was thinking and watching. She hoped no customer would disturb her thoughts. "What if Mark borrowed money just so he could buy something from *me?* And what if he came on to Rhonda even though he wasn't interested in her? I'm getting that feeling again. That Mark likes *me.*"

After work Meg rushed home to call Rhonda. She told her everything. Rhonda stopped her near the end. "This Toolie wants to meet me? All right-o. He's neat. This is sounding perfect. Tomorrow the four of us will meet at Beefy Burg. We'll celebrate the end of your grind at Harriman's and the beginning of something beautiful between Toolie and me and you and Mark."

"Who says Mark is going to show up?"

"I sez. Now turn on *Tomorrow's Yesterday* and see what awaits you today's tomorrow. See you then. Twelve fifteen at Beefy Burg. In line, I guess."

"Okay. See you today's tomorrow," said Meg, and she hung up.

Meg turned on *Tomorrow's Yesterday.* She pretended that Mark was doing some of the things that Rick was doing on the program. But not all of them.

The doorbell rang. "Got it," yelled Meg. As usual her mother was busy in the kitchen.

Mrs. Gish was at the door. "This will not be unpleasant," she said right away. "As I told your mother over the telephone, I'm sorry I got a bit overheated the day I was here. The fact is, I want to join forces with your mother. She has a direct line to the unfortunates. I think we could work well together. I'd like to ask her to join the membership of YWMTYT."

"Come in," said Meg. She called to her mother. "Mom, you have a visitor."

Mrs. Lowman came into the front hall. Mrs. Gish repeated almost word for word what she had said to Meg.

"Would you like some tea?" asked Mrs. Lowman.

"That would be lovely," said Mrs. Gish.

Meg's mother poked Meg and smiled as Mrs. Gish walked ahead into the living room. Mrs. Gish was about five down on their problems list for the photography session. "She could mess it up for you, Mom," Meg had warned. "I don't know how, but she could."

Meg went back to her television program after she crossed Mrs. Gish off the list.

Rick wasn't on again. Meg felt disappointed.

19

"You'll never get another chance like this one," Toolie said to Mark. "It's a perfect setup. Meg and Rhonda, you and me at Beefy Burg. Meg knows you like her. She knows you borrowed money just to buy things from her. And I practically told her you don't care about Rhonda. *I* have a thing for Rhonda."

"You shouldn't have told her about the money. Bad enough if it was my own money, but to borrow it to do it—oh, man! You've just made the Flaw-Away disaster more of a disaster."

"Forget it. You just come along with me tomorrow and you can throw away that book forever."

"I'm supposed to be going with the flow."

"Good. Get yourself a boat and sail along to victory."

"No, really. That book is getting to me again. And when it says I'm supposed to be in my free and spontaneous period, well it means it. See, you and I are just a couple of high school kids. But that Dr. Hunter has lived. People travel to see him and get his advice. Isn't that what we do every day of the school year? Listen to someone who's supposed to know more than we do?"

"But our teachers don't wear open shirts so their chest hair shows. Come on. Go with me tomorrow."

"I'll meet you there. At twelve fifteen. In line."

"Are you sure?"

"Just about."

The next day Toolie walked over to the end of the line at Beefy Burg at quarter past twelve. Meg and Rhonda were already there. Meg was smiling. She handed Toolie a fistful of money. "It was a snap," she said. "Ms. Selwyn and Mrs. Cogshell actually kissed me when I left. I felt kind of sad."

"You're great," said Toolie. He turned to Rhonda. "And you're Rhonda. Hi, Toolie here."

"Hi, Toolie. Is that your real name?"

"No. My real name is Max, but I've been called Toolie ever since I can remember. It comes from something cute and adorable I did or said when I was a baby, but my parents have forgotten what it was."

Meg was listening quietly. How easy it was for Rhonda and Toolie. Hitting it off, just like that. But where was Mark? She didn't want to ask Toolie. No one had said he was coming. It was only Rhonda's prediction.

"I'm buying," said Toolie as the line inched forward. "It's the least I can do now that I'm rich again."

Now Rhonda was looking around for Mark. "Your friend Mark. By chance, is he coming?"

"By chance he is," said Toolie. "He should be here any second."

Rhonda made a knowing face at Meg.

At twelve thirty they were almost up to the counter. No one said anything. The three of them seemed engaged in a silent vigil. At quarter to one they slid into a booth with their food. Toolie and Rhonda slid in side by side, which left Meg sitting alone opposite them. She was facing the entrance. She wondered if they did it that way so that she could watch for Mark. The orange Formica table in front of her was greasy and full of crumbs. Unopened packets of ketchup and mustard were sitting in the crumbs. The packets were shaped like animals. There was a hippo ketchup and a rhino ketchup, and lion and tiger mustard. "Beefy Burg must be making a pitch for big-game hunters or anyone under two," Meg thought as she opened a rhino by decapitating him. She was not in a good mood.

"*This* was worth waiting for?" asked Toolie.

"It's worse at Healthburgers," said Rhonda. "Ever seen a leftover avocado?"

They started to eat their Beefy Burgs and drink their strawberry shakes. Rhonda and Toolie talked to each other between bites. Meg was left with the Mark vigil. Not that she wanted it. No one mentioned his name. He was like someone banished from their civilization. But at quarter past one Toolie said, "Guess he got a little busy." He whispered under his breath, "the jerk."

"Say it louder," said Meg.

20

"You idiot. You blew it!" said Toolie. He stormed into Mark's house. "I'm going to throw away that book. Look, I've got my money back. I'll *buy* it from you. Then I'll throw it away."

"It wasn't the book," said Mark. "Well, it was and it wasn't. I'm supposed to be going with the flow, using my own instincts, and all of that. So I did and that's why I stayed home. I couldn't face her across the table. She knows too much about . . . about what I did. I made this decision myself, from my own feelings, even though the book told me to use my own feelings."

"That book is evil, I'm convinced of it. If it weren't for the book, you'd have used *different* feelings and you'd have shown up."

"I don't get what you're saying."

"Neither do I. I'm just mad."

"How did it go with Rhonda?"

"It went terrific. I've never met any girl with so much personality."

"What about Meg? She's got everything."

"This is so pathetic. You're hung up on her and she was hung down on you. You should have seen her. She was depressed when you didn't show up."

"Did she say so?"

"She wouldn't come out and say it. She's got pride."

"So have I. And that's why I didn't show up."

"So what next?"

"I'm going to give the book one last try."

"Why did I know you were going to say that? Well, I'm going to give the telephone a try. I'm calling Rhonda to invite her to the All-City Dance. It's in two weeks. I couldn't ask her in front of Meg."

"That dance? They have it every year. Guess they're trying to keep us kids off the street."

"Yeah. For one night."

After Toolie went home, Mark went into the kitchen and ate lunch. He was thinking about the lunch with Meg he could have had at Beefy Burg. He would never know how it would have turned out. But how could he have shown his face? Meg knew all about him . . . all of the wrong things. If only she could see him as someone desirable and exciting.

Mark ate a tuna sandwich while he read a new chapter of *How to Meet a Gorgeous Girl*. He couldn't find anything to fit his situation. He kept reading. Finally he was at Chapter Eleven. By Chapter Eleven, the guy is supposed to be in control. He is in a totally successful situation. The gorgeous girl is now madly in love with him. He needs just a bit more advice—to be found in

Chapter Twelve—to clinch everything. Chapter Twelve was called "Finishing Touches." Mark read it. But all that success was giving him a stomachache. Dr. Hunter wasn't writing about flops at this point. You could flop in the beginning or in the middle or even three quarters of the way through, but not in Chapter Twelve. Mark had a dumb, sick feeling that he had somehow disappointed Dr. Hunter. All that enthusiasm, all that encouragement for nothing. Couldn't he have one last chance?

Yes! Mark was feeling hopeful again. He could turn the pages back. There was no law that said you had to read a book strictly from front to back, and then close it forever. Maybe he had missed something vital earlier in the book, when he was allowed to be unsuccessful. Mark flipped pages backward. A sentence leaped out at him. "Make yourself wanted." He read the sentence again. Then he read the entire paragraph:

Make yourself wanted. Think of yourself as the coveted one and you will *be* the coveted one. Sounds simplistic? It isn't. Think of yourself as a diamond ring in a store window. Price tag in the thousands. People stop. They stare at you. They want you. They see you as something above them, an unreachable goal. And they want you more and more. *Become* that unreachable goal and watch the girls flock around you! Watch *the* girl want *you!!!*

"How do I become an unreachable goal?" Mark wondered. He flipped more pages, forward and backward. But he couldn't find anything else. "Well, I'm a diamond ring, now what? Just being something in a store window isn't going to do it. Unreachable, unreachable . . ."

Mark closed the book. "Nuts to Dr. Hunter! Who does he think I am? This is so dumb. I can't become unreachable. He may as well tell me to turn green. There *are* a few unreachable kids in school, but they didn't get there through any advice book."

Mark thought of Bonnie Packelberry. She was the most unreachable person he had ever seen. Guys flocked around her. She could have her pick. She was the diamond of Portland High School. The most popular girl. Getting a date with her could put *him* in the same league. "But she's not my type," thought Mark. "Flashy. Bold. Still . . ."

Mark saw himself at the All-City Dance with Bonnie Packelberry. Two diamonds together. Maybe Meg would see them there, glittering in unison. She would see him as the star he really was. She would want him.

What if he called Bonnie? What if he invited her to the dance? She would turn him down of course. He didn't really care. It was just a long shot. His ego wasn't in it. How simple it was when you didn't care!

Mark found Bonnie Packelberry's number in the telephone book. There was only one Packelberry listed. He dialed the number quickly.

"Fast is better," he thought. "Fast keeps you from knowing what you're doing."

"Hello." The voice was soft and sexy. It didn't want to let go of *hello*.

"Is this Bonnie Packelberry?"

"Who wants to know?"

"Me. My name is Mark Gardner. I go to Portland High."

"Uh huh."

"How are you?"

"Well just fine. How are you?"

"Just fine, too. I was thinking that if you weren't busy —that is, I know you're always busy, but just if you weren't busy one particular night, I'd like to invite you to go to the All-City Dance with me. You know, that's the dance that's held each year at one high school or the other and every high school kid in the city is invited. This year it's being held in our high school gym."

"I know all about it."

"I guess that means you're already going with somebody."

"Well, I'd love to go with *you*."

"*Me?*"

"Yes. You're inviting me, aren't you? Isn't that what you just did?"

"Sure!"

"Well, I'm accepting."

"Super! Can I pick you up at about, well, is eight o'clock convenient? If it isn't, I can come at quarter to eight or quarter past eight or seven thirty or eight thirty. Name a time."

"Eight o'clock is just wonderful."

"Then we'll see each other then."

"We sure will."

"Well, good-bye for now."

"Good-bye for now."

Mark hung up. "Yahoo! She knew me! She wants to

go out with me! If only Meg Lowman could have heard that conversation. Both ends of it. Well, she'll see the result if she's at the dance, and that's even more important."

Mark tried to toss the telephone book high in the air, but it was too heavy.

"Dr. Hunter doesn't know about Bonnie Packelberry. I did this one without him. I think I'm getting weaned."

21

Mrs. Lowman's cookbook was materializing. A contract was being drawn up between her and Preston House Press. Mr. Goodwin was telephoning frequently. He planned to send rough illustration sketches for Mrs. Lowman's approval within two months. They had decided which recipes would be included and which ones would be put aside. "Perhaps for your next book," Mr. Goodwin had said. This caused another round of frenzy in the Lowman household. Preston House Press was sending a photographer in about ten days to take the cover photo.

"Are you sure we can pull it off?" Meg's mother kept asking her.

"Sure we can."

"I wish your father were here."

"No, you don't," said Meg. "Unless you can keep him out of his closet."

"I invited Grandma Seeny over to watch the photo

session. But she turned me down. Can you believe it?"

"Yep. How's Augie?"

"Attentive. Very attentive."

"That's what I thought. You still owe him a meal. Did you forget about that one?"

"How could I?"

"You have a point. What are you going to do about it?"

"I'm going to take one meal at a time."

"You're turning into a philosopher, Mom. That's cool."

"Not very. Grandma Seeny and Augie are coming over tonight. They invited themselves. They're coming in Augie's car."

"Oh, no! How are you going to handle it when she finds out we've been giving her the ride-around?"

"I haven't the vaguest."

"Are they eating supper here?"

"Yes. And speaking of meals, remember that breakfast . . ."

"Here we go again. Mom, you keep reminding me. I don't want to talk about it."

"But I can't help wondering whatever happened to that nice boy. How come you haven't been going out with him? You haven't been turning him down, have you?"

"He's an idiot," said Meg.

"You're really stuck on him, huh?"

"Mom!"

"Well, I met him and he certainly isn't an idiot. Maybe a bit shy."

"Shy? That'll be the day. Can we change the subject?"

"Of course. But I'd like to see you have some kind of social life. You turned down too many boys last winter. You scared them off. They might have come in handy this summer."

"They didn't appeal to me. I'd rather study than go out with boring boys. I'd rather do nothing. Can't help it. That's the way it is. Rhonda's been bugging me to go to this All-City Dance with her and this guy who's a pal of this so-called nice boy. But I don't want to be the third person. And I'm not crazy about going alone. They say lots of kids go alone, but . . . I don't know."

"Go," said Mrs. Lowman.

"I told Rhonda I'd think about it, and I will. I don't like dances. You stand around and pretend you're talking to a girlfriend, but you've really got your mind on whether anyone is going to ask you to dance. It's meant to be a party with everyone mingling, but it doesn't work out that way. They should hang Choose Me Please signs around the girls' necks at the admission door. And you even have to pay admission. I hate the idea of that. But it keeps out the crashers, I guess."

Mrs. Lowman put her hand on Meg's arm.

"I hear a car. They're here!"

"Who?"

"Grandma Seeny and August."

"Oh, I forgot about them. This might get sticky. How can I help?"

"*Please*, just be here." Her mother smiled at her.

Meg liked the idea of her mother depending upon her. Somebody needed her, felt close to her, had a relationship with her. Nothing could ever replace her mother.

The doorbell rang and the door opened. Grandma Seeny let herself in. "He's a genius!" she said.

August Knotts followed, smiling.

"Who's a genius?" Meg asked.

"Augie, of course. He's a navigational genius. Does he ever know his way around town! Guess how long it took us to get over here. Guess!"

August Knotts kept smiling.

Meg hoped her mother wouldn't have an attack of hysteria. Funny hysteria or anxiety hysteria. Either was possible.

Meg said, "Um, well, let's see . . . about . . . about . . ."

Grandma Seeny couldn't wait. "Five minutes! I timed it. I looked down at my watch when we left. I wanted to allow a good half hour to get here. But it only took him five minutes!"

"That's wonderful, August." Meg's mother was beaming.

"I don't like to say anything, and no offense to you, Trish, but men know their way around," said Grandma Seeny. "I think it's some kind of natural instinct with them. Nothing for you to be ashamed of."

"I'm not," said Meg's mother. "Sit down and I'll get both of you a congratulatory drink."

"I'm going upstairs and change," said Meg. "I'll be back."

Meg hummed as she went upstairs and changed her clothes.

"There's joy in the Lowman household tonight," she thought. "And I feel recharged. Mom and I are having fun. Dad will be home in ten days. I'm looking forward to that. Mark Gardner no longer exists in my universe. I've stopped watching *Tomorrow's Yesterday*. I'm disgusted with Rick. I cleaned up my summer nicely."

The telephone rang. Meg answered it on the extension in her room.

"It's me," said Rhonda on the other end. "With another plea. I'm getting tired of being a supplicant. So please say you'll go to the All-City Dance."

"Oh, sure. Without a date."

"But most of the kids won't have dates. Guys will come over and ask you to dance. I guarantee it."

"The meat market. The lineup."

"Oh, come on. It's at Portland High. It's a chance to meet kids from another school and from around town."

"Like I met Mark Gardner? Forget I said that. I'll think about it. But I'm not going with you and Toolie, like a hangnail. And don't talk about me to Toolie. Don't tell him you asked me to go with you. Don't *discuss* me at all."

"I won't. I promise."

Mark Gardner was asking himself why he called Bonnie Packelberry. "I wanted a diamond and I got it. There's no one flashier than Bonnie Packelberry. What if I'm doing all of this for nothing? What if Meg just doesn't turn up at the dance? But she's so gorgeous someone will ask her. This is the last thing I'll ever do for Dr. Hunter. I'll make myself wanted, I'll be a diamond for one night, but that's it."

"Who is Mark Gardner?" Bonnie Packelberry was asking herself over and over. "Oh, well, it doesn't matter. It was getting to be a drag turning everybody down. I can't hope forever that Ken will be back in town in time to take me to that dance. This guy Mark is living and breathing and has a great sense of timing. He called at the right moment." Bonnie waltzed around the room. "Another guy madly in love with Bonnie Packelberry. They're dropping like flies. Becoming a dumb blonde was the smartest thing I ever did. Mark whatever his last name is, I'm forgetting it already, is one lucky guy. I wonder if my roots need a touch-up."

22

Cleaning up Randolph, Charlie, and Burt for the photo session was an awesome job.

"We have to respect *their* standards," Meg's mother said to her. "Just because *we* want them to have a certain look doesn't mean it's right for *them*. But I've explained to them that this is just a one-time thing that has to be done to meet the publisher's standards. I'm doing my part. I'm dressing in my most attractive outfit."

"But they're dressing in Dad's most attractive outfits," said Meg. "And he doesn't know it."

"Well, it would have been expensive and ridiculous to explain everything and ask his permission on a transoceanic telephone call. Getting through to tell him I was getting a cookbook published was enough. Besides, your father has plenty of spare clothes."

Meg watched while Randolph, Burt, and Charlie made their selections from her father's closet. Her mother turned various rooms of the house into private dressing rooms so they could try on the clothes. The suits were too big, too small, and much too small on Charlie, Burt, and Randolph respectively. The shirts were wrong, too, but they only showed around the collar. The ties were fine. "We'll skip shoes," said Mrs. Lowman. "Who looks down?"

But people look up, Meg was thinking. Charlie, Burt, and Randolph had sparse, unkempt hair that sprouted in several directions. It was the same kind of hair many intellectuals had. Safe enough. Her father certainly didn't have any spare hair to contribute.

Her mother hadn't mentioned the word bath. But Randolph, Burt, and Charlie arrived freshly clean for the photo session. Her mother was touched by that. Obviously they wanted to please her.

Mrs. Lowman was trying just as hard for herself. "Do you have any of that Flaw-Away stuff around?" she asked Meg.

"Sorry. It's back in stock at Harriman's. But you look fine. Besides, maybe they'll only get the back of your head. Think about it. It's a round table. The picture can't show everyone head-on."

"The back of my head? Oh, I never thought about that. How does it look?"

"Nice."

"Is that the doorbell?"

"No. Don't be so nervous. She'll come."

"What if she doesn't?"

"Mom, they promised you a well-groomed lady for a diner, right? Someone in the soup kitchen has been looking for the right type for a couple of weeks. They even promised they'd drive her to your house. So what's the problem?"

"The problem is that I don't know who 'they' are. The employees at the soup kitchen keep changing, and the director is hardly ever around. And we must be careful not to call it a soup kitchen. Mrs. Gish got them to rename it The Snackerie."

"How adorable."

"The more pressure she puts on other aspects of her YWMTYT project, the less she bugs me. She was here again one day while you were out. I hope she doesn't get to be a habit. Not that she's nasty. She gives a very low-keyed lecture about worth and that's it."

Mrs. Lowman looked in the mirror again.

"Come on, Mom. Let's join the fellows. It's not right having them sit around the table like that, just waiting. It's tough for them, too."

"I'm set," said Mrs. Lowman. "And the lunch looks beautiful. We mustn't forget the lunch. The art director and I picked out the most colorful-looking menu right over the phone."

Meg and her mother went into the dining room. Meg tried to see the scene the way a camera would. Randolph, Charlie, and Burt were sitting around the table in their regular chairs. They looked stiff. They looked ill-dressed. They looked ill. But the total effect wasn't too bad. Two scientists and a judge are not supposed to be fashion experts. They're supposed to be thinking people. Who would Central Casting have sent? Maybe the same types. After all, Randolph had been a real judge and maybe Burt and Charlie were real scientists. Meg didn't know that they *weren't*. She and her mother simply hadn't believed that they were. If you didn't think about it too much, the scene was absolutely authentic.

The doorbell rang. "She's here!" Mrs. Lowman said. She rushed to the door. Everyone looked toward the door. Here was the woman who would be permanently seated at the table on the cover of *The Cookbook of the Five Diners*.

Mrs. Lowman opened the door.

Mrs. Carter Gish walked in.

"Oh, no!" said Mrs. Lowman by way of greeting.

"I'm not going to make a scene," said Mrs. Gish. "I simply want to know one thing. Are you paying these gentlemen to be your models in this commercial endeavor?"

"They're not models. They're real," said Meg.

Mrs. Lowman looked at Meg. Neither of them had ever thought of paying the men. Mrs. Lowman had served them meal after meal. Wasn't that payment? Maybe it wasn't.

"Understand," said Mrs. Gish, as she stepped inside, "I've come to respect the primary need of food in a hungry stomach. But a crisp check in your hand is a gift of esteem."

"I hadn't thought about it that way," said Mrs. Lowman. She looked at Meg. Meg shrugged.

"I'll pay them," said Mrs. Lowman.

"How much?" asked Mrs. Gish.

"Are you their agent?" asked Meg.

"Somebody has to be," said Mrs. Gish.

"I'll take it up with my publisher," said Mrs. Lowman. "If they don't pay for this sort of thing, I will. I really will."

"I believe you," said Mrs. Gish. She turned to Randolph, Charlie, and Burt. "Did you hear that, gentlemen?"

They nodded.

Mrs. Gish turned to leave. "Well, I won't bother you. The people at The Snackerie are very excited about your project. And I personally am beginning to feel that something of worth may be coming out of it."

"Thank you," said Mrs. Lowman. Then her eyes widened. Mrs. Gish was standing in the open doorway. Beyond her, Mrs. Lowman could see a photographer with his equipment coming up the walk.

He strolled into the house. "Danny Slaughter," he said, extending his hand to Mrs. Lowman. "Make it Danny."

Meg's mother shook his hand. She said, "You're early." Then she introduced Meg and Mrs. Gish. "My daughter Meg and Mrs. Gish."

"Hi," said Danny. Then he peered into the dining room. He turned back to Mrs. Gish. "You must be the fourth diner. Take off your coat and stay awhile. I gotta admit I'm in awe of you fancy wine-tasting types. I've always wanted to live that rarefied kind of existence but I'm stuck with mundane photography."

Mrs. Gish pressed her lips together. Something in her face twitched.

Danny kept talking. "Let's see what we got here. Which one's the judge and which two are the scientists? Let me guess. I'm great at character studies. That's part of my trade."

Danny went into the dining room with his equipment. Meg closed the front door quickly and said in a low voice to Mrs. Gish, "You want worth, you've got it.

The fourth diner didn't show. We need you. Without you, these guys get no paychecks. Who knows, maybe this will lead to something else for them. It's a hope. A little one, but it's there."

Meg stared at Mrs. Gish. Was Mrs. Gish just a credo-spouting phony or was she a compassionate person?

Mrs. Gish hesitated. Her lips came unstuck. They formed a faint smile. She took off her coat.

Danny set up lights and rearranged drapes. He removed a vase from a sideboard. "You can't have a vase growing out of someone's head," he said. He played with different angles. Finally he decided that Mrs. Gish would be in the center face-on. She didn't seem to mind.

"She's fantastic," Meg thought. Mrs. Gish not only sat patiently for the picture taking but complimented the appearance of the food and conversed with the men as if they were all friends. She knew quite a bit about wine. Meg wondered if Danny noticed that Burt and Charlie didn't talk like scientists. Randolph was fine. He told a couple of courtroom stories while everyone pretended to eat. They weren't supposed to touch the food until the photo session was over. Meg kept watching her mother. Her mother was nervous but close to ecstatic that everything had worked out perfectly. She could see an actual friendship forming between her mother and Mrs. Gish. "You just can't tell about anything," Meg thought.

The doorbell rang.

"Who can that be?" said Mrs. Lowman. "Maybe it's a neighbor. I'll make it brief."

"I'll take it, Mom," said Meg. Her mother seemed to be in a cloudlike trance. Meg wasn't. She had a good idea who was on the other side of the door. She opened it. A woman was standing there.

"We aim to please from The Snackerie," said the woman. Then she waved away a car that was in front of the house while she stepped inside.

Meg looked at her. She had red hair, a red face, and a red dress that looked as if it had gone the full fifteen rounds in a prizefight. She was carrying a shopping bag with a pillow, a candlestick, and one shoe sticking out of it. And she was wearing cat box filler perfume.

But she was polite. "Sorry I'm late," she said, as she stepped into the dining room.

23

"Have you decided?" Meg's mother asked her. "Are you going to the All-City Dance?"

"Maybe I'll decide tomorrow," said Meg.

"But the dance is tonight."

"Exactly."

"Okay. I've never been a pushy mother, and I won't start now. But you've been mooning around the house lately. I think your one bright spot was when the lady in red showed up. It was just ghastly, but you perked right up."

"Well, I had to do something. I couldn't let her wreck it for you."

"But saying 'We already have an Avon lady and we're loyal to her' and then hustling the woman out of the house, that was so inspired."

"And so costly," said Meg. "She was pretty inspired herself. Before I got her out the door she whispered, 'Money and food.' What could I do? It wasn't all that terrible taking her to a nice restaurant. She *was* entitled to lunch. And paying for a taxi for her afterwards was okay, too. But when she asked me for a twenty-dollar bill so she could tip the driver, well, that got to be a little much."

The telephone rang. "It's Rhonda," said Meg. "I know it's Rhonda making a last-ditch plea for me to go tonight."

Meg answered the telephone. "Hello, Rhonda."

"Is that an insult?" asked Rhonda. "Like I'm bugging you? Well, I'm not. I've been thinking it over. You shouldn't go to the dance tonight because you don't want to."

"At last, the voice of reason."

"Yeah, those dances are pretty dumb, anyway. The band's always third-rate, the mosquitoes usually crash, and the refreshments taste like dog chow rejects. If Toolie hadn't asked me, I wouldn't go. I'd rather go to a concert or something."

"Yeah."

"Oh, well, what can I do? I *have* to go. But you don't. Well, talk to you tomorrow."

"Okay."

Meg hung up. "Rhonda has an educational deficiency," she thought. "She's never heard of overkill. Why didn't she stop while she was winning. Something's up. She's too anxious for me to stay away from that dance. Could it have something to do with Mark? She's got me curious, and I don't want to be."

Rhonda put down the telephone receiver. "Score a big one for Rhonda Schwartz," she thought. "I promised Meg I wouldn't discuss her with Toolie. And I didn't. But can I help it if Toolie called me today and dropped the unsolicited information that Mark is taking the wow girl of their high school to the dance? That's all Meg has to see. Well, if you can't save your closest friend from pain, what's it all about? I talked her right out of going. But I sure hate achieving success by being so slick and smooth."

Bonnie Packelberry liked her new dye job. "It's the real me," she said, fluffing her hair. "Platinum Packelberry. Now I've got the whitest hair in school. I'll wear my white sweater and my white pants tonight to go with it. A smash. The only flaw in the evening is I don't know who I'm going out with. First name Mark. Or was it Art? I already forget his last name. What if he's a creep or something? His only known talent is that he's a master of good timing. He called just when my Ken vibes were fading. I turned down four guys before him and three guys after he invited me. He'd better be better than those seven guys. What if he wrecks my image? I've invested two years in it. You don't get to be the Marilyn Monroe of Portland High School just by wishful thinking. Art, whatever your name is, you'd better deserve me."

Mark Gardner put *How to Meet a Gorgeous Girl* back into his bookcase. "I don't need it anymore," he thought. "When I see what a snap it was for me to get a date with the most popular girl in school . . . well, I've been underestimating myself all along. I could have asked Meg for a date in the very beginning and she would have fallen all over herself saying yes. That first day at the cosmetics counter I could have sealed my future.

"I guess.

"Instead of saying, 'I need a face blusher for my sister,' I could have said, 'How about going out with me?' She would have said, 'When?' and that would have been that. I'm so much greater than I thought I was. If I actually *had* a sister, she could have told me that as she would have seen me from a girl's point of view.

"But I don't have a sister. I can't be sure of anything. Why would a person like Bonnie Packelberry accept a person like me? She sounded alert and sane, and the telephone connection was clear and I don't think anyone was holding a gun to her head when she said yes, because people who are being threatened try to give out a warning with a code word or something.

"No, it was all normal, and I did it myself. That Dr. Hunter, what does he know? In private I bet he calls all the girls chicks. I should never have taken advice from a marked-down psychoanalyst who probably gets the hair on his chest permanented regularly."

Meg Lowman finished supper quickly. She went to her room and put on a brown shirt and blue jeans. "Good enough for a dance in a gym," she decided.

24

Mark didn't want to call Bonnie Packelberry back to get directions to her house. It wasn't on a major street like Meg's house. It would be hard to find. But what if Bonnie said "Get lost"? A girl as popular as that could say almost anything and get away with it. But of course she wouldn't say that to him because she was so enthusiastic about going out with him. "She must have noticed me at school," Mark thought. "And I didn't notice her noticing. I wonder how many unknown, unconsummated crushes on Mark Gardner there are out there in the halls of Portland High. Dozens maybe. It's a staggering thought, but I have to live with it."

Bonnie Packelberry lived in a house that was surprisingly not much different from all the other houses in the neighborhood. Her neighborhood and her street had been easy to find after asking directions only twice along the way. Mark walked up the front steps of her house.

"This house isn't jazzy or flashy or anything," Mark thought. "It's kind of plain and dull. Her parents could be reclusive. Girls like Bonnie Packelberry often spring from reclusive parents."

Mark rang the doorbell. "I hope she doesn't keep me waiting on this porch. The book says that being kept waiting is a major confidence killer. Like watching your hair frizz or stubble grow on your chin."

Mark waited. "Then again, the book says that sometimes girls keep you waiting on purpose because *they're* insecure. If they rush to open the door, you might be able to witness their insecurity in one quick blast. I would never have thought that Bonnie Packelberry was insecure, but, well, here's the proof. Wait till I tell Toolie."

Mark continued to wait. "Maybe the doorbell doesn't work. It could be one of those broken doorbells that you can hear on the outside but not on the inside. A doorbell like that could break up a relationship before it even starts. I'll count to sixty, and then I'll ring again. Sixty seconds is one minute, and that's a good basic unit of time."

Mark counted to sixty. "Well, I guess I should ring again. But what if she's in there rushing around, doing those last-minute things that contribute to making her the most popular girl in Portland High School. I wouldn't want to stop her in her momentum."

The door opened. An elderly man stood in the doorway. "Who are you?" he asked.

"I'm a friend of Bonnie's. I mean I'm taking her to the All-City Dance."

"You are?"

"Yes. My name is Mark Gardner and I go to Portland High School. I know Bonnie from school. That's where I know her from."

Mark was remembering a warning from the book. *Establish your respectability before you pick her up.* The book was referring to picking up an unknown girl on a street corner, but it certainly couldn't hurt in this situation.

"Come in," said the man. He was thin and slightly bent over. His hair was white and thin. He looked like somebody's grandfather.

Mark always did well with grandfathers and grandmothers. For example, Toolie's grandparents were wild about him. Mark knew he was in what the book called *a compatible situation.* Mark was surprised that he was recalling so many things from the book, especially since he had decided he didn't need it anymore. But it was all coming in handy.

"You must be Bonnie's grandfather," he said.

"Father."

"Oh."

"How long have you known Bonnie?"

"Well, we've been going to the same school for two years."

"That's not the same as knowing."

Mark was beginning to wonder how Bonnie could have become so popular if everyone had to get through this palace guard to go out with her.

He heard a rustling sound. He looked in back of him and up. There was Bonnie coming down the stairs! She was wearing a white sweater and white, tight satin pants. Her hair was almost white, too. Wasn't her hair usually yellow? Maybe under the gym lights it would look yellow, Mark hoped. He had never before been out on a date with a white-haired person.

When Bonnie reached the bottom of the stairs, she stopped and looked Mark over as if she were seeing him for the first time. Suddenly Mark realized she *was* seeing him for the first time. She didn't have the vaguest idea who he was! Why had she accepted the date?

All at once Mark had what the book called *total cognizance of a situation in which you find yourself with a girl.* That meant you knew just what she was all about. What Bonnie was about, Mark realized, was being the prototype flake. She had the *four Fs,* as the book described them. She was *flirty, freaky, fickle* and *flaky.* But the book said you could have a real good time with a girl like that. He wondered how many guys at Portland High had had a real good time with a girl like that.

"Hi," said Bonnie. "You must be, uh . . ."

She couldn't remember his name, first or last.

"Mark Gardner," said her father wearily.

"Oh, Daddy, you're always filling in boys' names!"

Mark rolled his eyes upward.

"Well, we're off to the dance, aren't we, uh . . ." She stopped.

"Mark," said her father.

They started toward the door.

"When will you be home?" asked her father.

"Early," said Mark.

"How early?"

"Possibly very," said Mark.

Outside under a street light Mark saw that Bonnie's

hair looked whiter than inside. There would be no hope for it under the gym lights.

"Do you mind walking?" asked Mark. "I'm working on my driver's license permit, but I don't have it yet."

"You're not a senior?"

"No, I'm just starting my junior year."

"You didn't tell me that when you asked me out."

"Is that important? *You're* not a senior."

"I know that. But like, seniors are more mature. Do you shave?"

"I've been shaving for years."

"Well, thank goodness for *that!*"

They passed under another street light. Mark wanted to close his eyes, but he was afraid he might trip.

25

Meg bought her ticket at the door to the gym. Some of her girlfriends whom she hadn't seen all summer came up to her. They were milling around the door. Some were buying tickets, some were just standing around, whispering to one another and trying to make up their minds what to do. One girl, Janet, said to Meg, "The ratio is three girls to every guy. We've been counting."

"I'm not staying long," said Meg. "I'm just looking around. It's a chance to see some of the kids I haven't seen since June. Like you. How's it going?"

"It's going boring. This was the worst summer yet."

"No, last summer was worse," said Lorna, who was with Janet. "How was your summer, Meg?"

"I worked for two months at Harriman's—just mornings—and the second month was great."

Meg was talking to Janet and Lorna, but her eyes were fixed in back of them. She was watching the door to the outside. She saw Rhonda and Toolie come in and walk toward her.

"Excuse me," Meg said to Janet and Lorna. She walked up to Rhonda and Toolie.

"What are you *doing* here! I told you not to come," said Rhonda.

"So it was true," thought Meg. "Rhonda was definitely trying to keep me from coming. But *why?* I can't ask with Toolie standing right there. I have a hunch I'll find out soon enough."

Meg went into the gym with Rhonda and Toolie. Whatever awaited her tonight would be easier to take with Rhonda and Toolie by her side.

Meg looked around. There were kids dancing and kids not dancing. Groups of them were leaning against the gym walls, eating, talking, laughing, and surveying the scene. There were a few mildly surprising combinations of couples. The music was terrible. It was all very nothing.

Rhonda and Toolie seemed afraid to leave her by herself. Toolie got punch for all of them. He handed a cup to Meg just as Mark Gardner walked into the gym with Bonnie Packelberry. So that was it, the reason why Rhonda hadn't wanted her to come tonight! Mark was here with a girl.

Who *was* this girl? That hair. Is she prematurely white? Is she diseased? Maybe it's his sister, the one who needed face blusher. This girl needs more than that. Or less than that. But look! A bunch of guys are going up to her already. Well, I don't care who she is. He can date the Statue of Liberty for all I care.

"There's Mark," said Meg matter-of-factly.

"Oh, is he here tonight?" said Rhonda.

"He's with someone."

"Oh, is he?" said Toolie.

"Over there."

Toolie turned toward the door. "That's Bonnie Packel-berry. She's kind of the most popular girl at our school. But she's not Mark's type."

"Then why did he invite her to the dance?"

"It's his way of chasing after you. I'm not supposed to tell you that, but, well, he's on his stupidity kick."

"Oh, c'mon. He invited her because he wanted to."

"No, the book wanted him to. See, he's got this book that gives advice. And he's been following the advice, no matter how nutty it is. I mean, this book cost two ninety-five and it's one of the all-time worst buys in history. It tells you how to get close to a person by moving in the opposite direction."

"I was so sure he liked me. But that day at Beefy Burg, I looked down at that Formica table and had my moment of truth. He didn't come. He could have, but he didn't. He disappeared from my life. Totally."

"But not in his head. See, he did some things that he thought you thought were dumb, and he was afraid to show his face. Now tonight he's really doing something dumb, but he thinks he's making an impression on you by being seen with *her*. One word in his favor. She had flashy blond hair, not flashy white hair, the last time I saw her. That part is new."

"I *told* you he liked you," said Rhonda. "I didn't know what he was up to, but I could sense he was hung up on you."

"Rhonda's hip," said Toolie. "I couldn't come out and tell her anything. It's Mark's business. I feel enough like a ratfink right now, spilling all this stuff to you."

Rhonda studied Bonnie. "I've seen ladies all in white before, but they carry thermometers and they keep cotton in the supply room, not on their heads."

"I'll see you guys later," said Meg.

Meg walked away before they could ask her where she was going. She started to walk toward the crowd around Bonnie Packelberry. She thought about what Toolie had told her. Mark and his far-out ideas! But was it any different, really, from what she and her mother had done, driving Grandma Seeny all around town? They should have leveled with Grandma Seeny from Day One. And what about Grandma Seeny blasting her radio and stereo in the hope of attracting "someone interesting." The things people do. Good motives. Bad execution. Whatever happened to just being direct? Simple. It takes guts. And it leaves you wide open. Who needs rejection and ridicule? But she wouldn't have rejected Mark. You're worth more than you think, Mark Gardner. And have I got an organization for you!

Meg kept walking toward Mark. He *liked* her. It was sinking in. Now she could admit to herself how much she liked him. She stopped and watched him from a distance.

Mark was slowly getting edged away from Bonnie. Or was he edging himself away? *That's* what he was doing! Stealthily he was moving away from her and allowing someone to step into his old space. When he saw Meg, he stopped. Meg walked forward.

"Excuse me," she said to the crowd around Bonnie. She pushed her way toward Mark.

"Hi, Meg," he said. "I want you to meet my date."

Mark tried to regain the territory he had just given up. "Bonnie!" He tried to grab her arm.

"Yes, Phil," she said.

"I'm Mark! *Mark!* Your father's smarter than you are."

Mark stepped back from Bonnie. He hit someone with his elbow. "Excuse me," he said. He got out of the crowd.

He walked up to Meg.

"I can explain her," he said. "She has to be explained."

"Her father sounds nice," said Meg.

"She's my date."

"Not anymore."

"She's the most popular girl in my high school."

"That doesn't say much for your high school."

"You mean that doesn't say much for me," said Mark.

"Mark, if you had asked *me* to the dance, I would have said yes. If you had asked me anywhere or did anything natural, up front, straight out, plain, no tricks, no Flaw-Away, no Glossy Glow, no Crinkle Concealer, I would have gone out with you."

"You would have?"

"I would have, and I will."

"No kidding?"

"No kidding."

"Who did you come with tonight?"

"Myself."

"I think I came with myself, too. Want to dance?"

"Sure."

Mark followed Meg out to the dance floor. Meg saw Rhonda and Toolie watching them. She waved to them. She knew she wouldn't have to ask Rhonda about Mark anymore. They would talk about him, sure. And she would have to write to Shari about him. But she wouldn't have to wonder about him. That was all over. Mark had made mistakes, but she had made some, too. She could have spoken up. She could have done something instead of just wondering about him. She could do something right now. Tomorrow was Sunday. "Want to come to breakfast tomorrow morning?" she asked. "I know Mom would love to have you, and I would, too."

"I'll be there!" said Mark.

At last it was happening to him! Everything he had hoped for since he first saw Meg behind the cosmetics counter at Harriman's Department Store was coming true. It was wonderful. More than that, it wasn't impossible. Simple questions. Simple answers. That's all it took. When he got home, he would throw the book away. Maybe he would cut out and save just one chapter. Right now he was experiencing what Chapter Four had called *the optimum moment*.

"If you don't blow it," the book had promised, "it could last forever."

"What are you thinking about, Mark?" Meg interrupted his thoughts.

For one instant he wondered what Dr. Hunter would have answered. Then suddenly he said, "Us," and he knew he was on his own.

ABOUT THE AUTHOR

MARJORIE SHARMAT spent her childhood in Portland, Maine. She began writing at age eight, when she and a friend published *The Snooper's Gazette*. Ms. Sharmat is the author of more than sixty books, and she and her husband make their home in Tucson, Arizona. Her most recent novels for Delacorte Press are *How to Meet a Gorgeous Guy* and *I Saw Him First*.